THE READER IN THE DICKENS WORLD

THE READER IN THE DICKENS WORLD

Style and Response

Susan R. Horton

University of Pittsburgh Press

First published in United Kingdom 1981 by
THE MACMILLAN PRESS LTD

Published in the U.S.A. 1981 by
the University of Pittsburgh Press
Pittsburgh, Pa., 15260

Printed in Great Britain

Library of Congress Cataloging in Publication Data

Horton, Susan R
  The reader in the Dickens world.

  Includes index.
  1. Dickens, Charles, 1812–1870—Criticism and interpretation. 2. Reader-response criticism.
  I. Title.
PR4581.H6   1981   823'.8   80-53031
ISBN 0-8229-1140-X

For

Richard L. Seibenick
and
Mildred R. Noneman Seibenick

'And that,' said I, 'is your deliberate opinion, Mr. Wemmick?'
'That,' he returned, 'is my deliberate opinion in this office.'
'Ah!' said I, pressing him, for I thought I saw him near a loophole
   here; 'but would that be your opinion at Walworth?'
'Mr. Pip,' he replied with gravity, 'Walworth is one place, and this
   office is another.'

Great Expectations

Contents

Note on the Texts   viii

Preface   ix

1   Introduction   1

2   Intention, Text and Response   4

3   Sequence and Consequence: from Truckling Knave to Trickling Blood   14

4   The Reader at Work   25
   1   The Rhetorics of Image and Idea   25
   2   Rhetoric and Plot   33
   3   The Reticent Rhetorician   41
   4   The Rhetoric of 'seems'   49

5   The World beyond the Dickens World   55
   1   Dickens's Peripheral Vision   55
   2   The Huddle   65
   3   The Double Vision   71
   4   The Time Telescope and the Labyrinth of the Conditional: the Expanding World in Time and Possibility   78

6   The Dynamics of Description   88
   1   Description as Re-creation   88
   2   Description as Defence   96
   3   Descriptions and Repetitions   99

7   One Reader Reading: the Reader in *The Old Curiosity Shop*   110

Notes   122

Index   132

Note on the Texts

ABBREVIATIONS

SB	*Sketches by Boz*
PP	*Pickwick Papers*
OT	*Oliver Twist*
NN	*Nicholas Nickleby*
OCS	*The Old Curiosity Shop*
BR	*Barnaby Rudge*
MC	*Martin Chuzzlewit*
DS	*Dombey and Son*
DC	*David Copperfield*
BH	*Bleak House*
HT	*Hard Times*
LD	*Little Dorrit*
TTC	*A Tale of Two Cities*
GE	*Great Expectations*
UT	*The Uncommercial Traveller*
OMF	*Our Mutual Friend*
MED	*The Mystery of Edwin Drood*

Page references are to volumes in *The Oxford Illustrated Dickens* (London: 1948–58). I have put all references to the novels in brackets after each quotation: book numbers in large Roman numerals, chapter numbers in small Roman numerals, page numbers in Arabic numerals. I have not referred to the pagination of the Clarendon editions of *Oliver Twist, Edwin Drood, Dombey and Son*, or *Little Dorrit*, because although those are fine and authoritative editions, I presume their cost prohibits their being part of the libraries of any but the most ardent Dickensians.

Preface

Subtitling a book 'Style and Response' might be regarded as evidence of either great naïveté or great audacity, as the briefest survey of representative critical position shows. After years of debate, we still are not sure either what 'style' is, or where it can be said to be present in a literary text. Even if and when we come to some agreement on where it is, we certainly do not begin to agree on what it does – to texts, to meanings, to readers – or even, as a matter of fact, if it does anything at all. Is style present where there is 'regularity' of language?[1] Or is it, contrarily, evident in the 'deviation from the norm'?[2] Roman Jakobson's by-now classic formulation for allowing us to recognise the 'poetic function', or style, in a text ('the poetic function projects the principle of equivalence from the axis of selection into the axis of combination')[3] gave us all a fine, sharp principle to hold on to as we went looking for style, but as Jonathan Culler noted in *Structuralist Poetics*, one can safely say that 'one has an instance of the poetic function only when one can point to effects which might be explained as the result of particular projections of the principle of equivalence from the axis of selection into the axis of combination'.[4]

Instead of beginning a search for style in and with the text, Culler would have us begin with ourselves and with our own responses to the text, then go back to the text to discover what linguistic patterns there had been at work in it that had caused those effects in us. Working backwards and inductively, we would arrive at a definition of and recovery of style.

This seems logical, rational, and promising. But two major difficulties remain to one who would talk about style and response. First, as Culler notes, 'even where linguistics provides definite and well-established procedures for classifying and describing elements of a text it does not solve the problem of what constitutes a pattern and hence does not provide a method for the discovery of patterns. *A fortiori*, it does not provide a procedure for the discovery of poetic patterns.'[5] The reader is thrown back upon his own sensitivity and common sense to discover where style is (it is present wherever I am affected by the text), but he is also thrown back on his own resources to generate a method for discovering those affective patterns, or perhaps even for generating the patterns themselves (depending upon whether I believe patterns are in texts, or in readers). The second major difficulty is revealed in Berel Lang's musings in a recent *Critical Inquiry* essay, in which he wonders whether 'the phenomenon of style – what stylistic categories categorise – is not perhaps a mode of personification and an end in itself rather than, as has more often been held to be the case, an instrumentality supposed to act on behalf of some other purpose'.[6]

Jakobson believes we can identify the poetic function, or style, in a literary text. Culler says that we have no method for discovering poetic patterns, and that we need to know what the effects of style are before we can find style in the first place. But Lang poses the possibility that style may be present only for its own sake, and may not necessarily be generating effects or meaning at all. The critic who would talk about 'style and response' is squeezed on all sides. It would seem to be time for some audacious – or naïve – stipulative definitions of terms like *style, pattern, effect* and *meaning* that will allow the critic some room and freedom in which to say something intelligent and interesting about particular literary works.

'Style', Berel Lang says, '*represents* the assertion of content.'[7] I like this definition, because it implies that wherever there is content, there is also style; and wherever there is style, there is also meaning. Jakobson tells a story in 'Linguistics and Poetics': a missionary blamed his African flock for walking undressed. 'And what about yourself?' They pointed to his visage. 'Are not you, too, somewhere naked?' 'Well, but that is my face.' 'Yet in us,' retorted the natives, 'everywhere it is face.' In this study, everywhere it is face.[8]

What style does and means are questions that can only be addressed and answered by an honest analysis of how the text strikes me as a reader. The texts are Dickens's. I find them rich, complex, various, as full of contradictions and multiplicities of meaning as life itself. With that perception, I have gone back to Dickens's texts to try to account for my perception of his works, and I have constructed patterns in his works to explain and account for my feelings about them. In doing so, I have indubitably and intentionally violated a usual critical practice. Critics are wont to talk about patterns of imagery; about symbolic patterns; about theme and vision. Ross Chambers suggests that the structuralist revolution, or more precisely the trend towards linguistic analysis of texts manifesting the so-called poetic function of language, has immeasurably increased our understanding of the types of relationships, paradigmatic and syntagmatic, which constitute the *'litérarité'* of texts. But it has necessarily left out of account those relationships which, because they are hierarchical, do not so easily admit of contrastive analysis in terms of binary equivalences; these are the 'interpreting relationships' which exist between a specific segment of discourse within a text and the text as a whole.[9]

I have taken this observation as an invitation to do something a bit different, but necessary, if I am to account for the meaning I think Dickens's texts bear. We usually combine image with image when we make statements of meaning. We stay on, in Professor Chambers's terms, one level or hierarchy when we interpret. I have not. I have patterned, for instance, not image with image, but image with rhetoric. I have assumed, as Seymour Chatman suggests in his new book *Story and Discourse*, that novels do not neatly divide into description, narration and commentary. Rather, description also provides implicit commentary; narration does as well.[10] In Dickens's novels, this implicit commentary that lies hidden in description often runs counter to the explicit commentary in the novels. I have needed to talk about image and rhetoric as if they were of the same hierarchical rung so that I could uncover the reason for my own rich responses to Dickens's novels.

Many of the separate observations of stylistic features that I shall make are not new. People have been comfortable talking for a hundred years, for instance, about the fact that Dickens's descriptions of characters often evoke the prospect of humans become beasts. They have claws and beaks; are chickens, snakes, eels, lynxes. I have combined these images, however, not with one another, but with the rhetoric that surrounds them. Doing this has resulted in the same old observations being turned into interpretations that are a bit different. 'The usual prelude to change' of an idea, an interpretation, a perception, or a theory, as Thomas Kuhn suggests in his Preface to *The Essential Tension*, 'is . . . the awareness of anomaly, of an occurrence or set of occurrences that does not fit existing ways of ordering phenomena. The changes [demand thinking in a new way], one that renders the anomalous lawlike, but that, in the process, also transforms the order exhibited by some other phenomena, previously unproblematic.'[11] Kuhn is talking here about the interpretation of scientific data. But what he says turns out to be true of literary interpretation as well. I began with a perception that Dickens's novels often felt contradictory. I have constructed patterns in them to explain the origin of my feelings about their contradictory nature. In the process I have necessarily transformed the previously · unproblematic – those images of people looking like beasts, for instance – into something somewhat more problematic than they had been before.

Except in my last chapter, I also connect not only across hierarchies, but across novels. My reader will not find in my table of contents the usual chapter on each novel, with an opening chapter on *Pickwick Papers*, and a conclusion on *The Mystery of Edwin Drood*. This is not because I don't believe in giving readings of novels – my last chapter is a reading of *The Old Curiosity Shop* – or because I see no change or development between Dickens's early and late novels, but because I am more interested in asserting those patterns and combinations and consequent effects that I see present and running through all of the novels. Finally, I believe what G. K. Chesterton said first and best:

> Dickens's work is not to be reckoned in novels at all. Dickens work is to be reckoned always by characters, sometimes by groups, oftener by episodes, but never by novels. You cannot discuss whether *Nicholas Nickleby* is a good novel, or whether *Our Mutual Friend* is a bad novel. Strictly, there is no such novel as *Nicholas Nickleby*. There is no such novel as *Our Mutual Friend*. They are simply lengths cut from the flowing and mixed substance called Dickens – a substance of which any given length will be certain to contain a given proportion of brilliant and of bad stuff.[12]

Whether brilliant or bad, Dickens's 'stuff' is always complex and contradictory, and every Dickens critic has had in one way or another to address that fact. Albert Guerard has done so in *The Triumph of the Novel*.[13] Barbara Hardy did it superbly in *The Moral Art of Charles Dickens*.[14] When Guerard says that Dickens's 'anal imagery and scenes which threaten engulfment, often find a counterweight in controlled syntax if not conversational calm',[15] he is responding to the kind of contradictions we all perceive. When Alexander Welsh in *The City in Dickens* talks about 'the variegation and cacophony of his surfaces implying some hidden moral disorder',[16] he is doing the same. None of us thinks that Dickens is confused; all of us perceive a richness of possibility for combining the separate elements of Dickens's world; all of us recognise, tacitly at least, that Dickens is different for different readers, depending upon the combinations and patterns critics and readers create out of that richness. 'The only works we value enough to call classic are those which . . . are complex enough to allow us our necessary pluralities,' says Frank Kermode, noting 'the extreme variety of response characteristic of the modern reading of the classic'.[17]

We all create our texts, as Albert Guerard makes disarmingly clear at the beginning of his book:

> My Dickens is the inventive fantasist and comic entertainer possessed of extraordinary narrative energy and creative power, rather than Leavis's 'serious thinker' and responsible social realist, or another's dark symbolist or a third's programmatic reformer.[18]

What follows, then, is an account of *my* Dickens. Coyly, perhaps, Wolfgang Iser once suggested that 'reality is a process of re-alisation'.[19] If what he meant was that each of us realises a text in one way rather than in another, what I might be allowed to say is that what will follow is the real – my real – Dickens.

I am, of course, all too keenly aware of how one assertion of meaning shuts out others; how one patterning precludes or obscures others; of how, as Stanley Fish says, 'declaratives create the conditions to which they refer.'[20] 'Any vigorous thought', says René Girard in 'Critical Reflections on Literary Studies', 'is sooner or later bound to arrive at its own bases; it will end, then, in reduction.'[21] This has happened to me, and the result is that this study, which began in 1971 as a book on Dickens, by some mysterious process of binary fission became two books in 1978, this one an analysis of stylistic effects in Dickens's novels, and the other an over-the-shoulder look at my own assumptions in generating and asserting the presence of those patterns and meanings. Those more theoretical speculations and explorations are to be found in my *Interpreting Interpreting: Interpreting Dickens's Dombey.*[22]

The author and publishers wish to thank Oxford University Press for permission to quote from *The Pilgrim Edition of the Letters of Charles Dickens.*

June 1979   S.R.H.

1 Introduction

Most critical remarks state in an abbreviated form that an object causes certain experiences, and as a rule the form of the statement is such as to suggest that the object has been said to possess certain qualities. But often the critic goes further and affirms that the effect in his mind is due to special particular features of the object. In this case he is pointing out something about the object in addition to its effect upon him, and this fuller kind of criticism is what we desire.[1]

There are some few writers and some few works of fiction that seem especially to fascinate generation after generation of critics. No matter how much is said of those works, they never seem to exhaust us, or we them. No matter how much we say about the work, the age, the writer, the style, and the relationships between and among these things, no matter how many structural, symbolic, and imagic patterns we trace in them, we are left with the feeling that a part of the essential meaning or significance we *feel* them to have has eluded our grasp. I have always felt this to be particularly true of the novels of Dickens. And I am not alone. Anyone who works his way through the last hundred years of Dickens criticism discovers that all of Dickens's critics, his contemporaries as well as modern critics, sooner or later begin to talk about Dickens's 'excess of energy', his 'energy of presentation', and about the 'echoes' or 'resonances' in his novels. What all of these words or phrases are, among other things, are recognitions and acknowledgements of the lack of correspondence or equivalence between our private responses to and our public critical pronouncements about Dickens's novels. Chesterton is acknowledging this gap when he says of Dickens's characters that the 'inside is always larger than the outside',[2] and we agree without hesitation, having very little if any real idea what those words might mean. Mario Praz called Dickens's characters 'more alive than life',[3] and we know what he means, too. E. M. Forster explains that Dickens's 'flat' characters can move us because they are moving by 'galvanic energy', the parts of the novel that are alive galvanising the parts that are not, thus making the characters appear to 'jump about and speak in a convincing way'.[4]

I am hardly interested in denigrating such honest attempts to construct rational analyses to account for and explain our emotional responses to Dickens's novels. Too often the naïve appreciator in us gets separated from the scholar-critic, and any effort at a re-integration of the two is one of the main tasks recent critics have set themselves to. In Dickens's case, the first step in that process has to be a putting of Dickens back together again. Historically, we have tended to dichotomise Dickens into a 'good' Dickens and a 'bad' Dickens. The first is an artistic genius who created hundreds of brilliantly conceived characters and intricately interwoven plots; the other is a hack who wrote bathetic melodrama and was given to rhetorical over-kill. We have submitted the former to analysis, the latter mostly to apology, in spite of the fact that we know the fullest criticism we could provide would analyse the whole. If rich and complex symbols are plentiful in the novels, so are the stumblings into the bathetic, and ultimately our responses to Dickens's creations must be assumed to be born out of both of these things; indeed, it will be my major point that the presence of the one affects our responses to the other, and vice versa. We have talked about Dickens's 'style' – his moral style, his comic style – as if it were possible to talk about Dickens's style in the singular in any book except one that would be called *Charles Dickens: The Protean Style*. Dickens wrote mystery stories in the style of the Gothic novel; descriptions that call up, by turns, a romance, a travelogue and a Faulkner novel; episodic narratives that belong in a picaresque tale; the oratory appropriate to a nineteenth-century sermon; the rhetoric of a Victorian periodical; the comedy, by turns, of an eighteenth-century play of humours, and a twentieth-century black humourist. And, further, he changed from one mode or style to another in the space of a paragraph.

So multiple is Dickens's style, and so various his language, that historically the temptation has been either to isolate and analyse the separate parts, conquering by division, or simply to surrender to the texts, exclaim and enjoy. The history of Dickens criticism has been a movement from one of these impulses to the other, and back again. I would like, however, to keep my eye on Dickens's multiple modes of presentation as much as or more than on his symbols or images or themes or plots alone, and I shall do so not merely in the interest of some kind of critical tidiness. In the process of asking why Dickens chose to write in such a multitude of modes, we can learn much about Dickens's intentions, and about his own responses to the world around him. In the process of balancing his intentions against his achievements, and discovering at what points his achievement seems to exceed his intentions and at what point his texts seem to do other than he intends, we can begin to uncover and understand, I think, the origin and causes for our own rich responses to the Dickens world.

Talking about not only a writer's intentions but about a reader's responses to those intentions as they are expressed in a literary text has become more respectable in recent years than it had been for a long while. Still, one who does it is destined to feel a bit like one who takes a walk through a demilitarised zone, expecting to be fired upon from any direction. Still, if talking about a writer's intentions and a reader's response leads me into perilous territory, the rewards, I think, are at least equal to the perils.

2 Intention, Text and Response

An important sentence in semiotics runs: within a system, the lack of one element is important in itself. If one applies this to literature, one will observe that the literary text is characterised by the fact that it does not state its intention, and therefore the most important of its element is missing. If this is so, then where is one to find the intention of a text? The answer is: in the reader's imagination.[1]

The literary text presents reactions to and attitudes toward the real world, and it is these reactions and attitudes that constitute the reality of a literary text.[2]

Charles Dickens's literary intentions, as he expressed them, were simple enough. He said again and again in his letters, his speeches, and in the Prefaces he wrote for various editions of his novels that he wanted to 'brighten up the lives and fancies of others'. He wanted to 'increase the stock of harmless cheerfulness' in the world; to tell his audience 'that the world is not utterly to be despised'. He wrote to please and to entertain. Being a writer for an audience whom John Butt and Kathleen Tillotson have described as 'delicately responsive'[3] to his every move, he was delighted each time he was smitten by what he often called 'a pretty idea', and always eager to see 'what effects' its execution would generate in his readers. Dickens found serial publication worth the headaches it gave him partly because that form allowed him to sample the reactions of his readers and to adjust his style and sometimes even his story in response to their opinions and preferences. When people whose judgement he respected, Lord Jeffrey or John Forster, for instance, expressed doubts about his treatment of some characters (Edith Dombey, Walter Gay, Pip and Estella), after consideration he changed the portrayal of those characters. When his audience responded favourably to his comedy, his pathos, his melodrama, his optimistic rhetorical and plot assurances of how the world was a good place and could be made better if people would only behave decently, being a popular pleaser he responded by creating more comedy, more pathos, more melodrama, more rhetorical assurances, more stories full of happy endings, as his audience requested.

What is most interesting to me, however, is what happens to Dickens's style as a result of the fact that both his own and his audience's demands and needs were contradictory. He was writing for a people who lived, as George Ford describes, 'looking backward to Regency high spirits, and forward to Victorian earnestness'.[4] They expected not only to be pleased and entertained, but were sure they ought to find some moral or lesson in books as well. When Thomas Carlyle reviewed Sir Walter Scott's novels, he was partly reflecting and partly generating the expectations and tastes of the times when he concluded that 'the Waverley novels were suitable family fare, to be sure, but what lessons did they teach?'[5] And there was still a further demand on the writer who would please a popular Victorian audience. The first twenty years of the nineteenth century in Britain had been marked by a terrible insensitivity in the laws it enacted. Penalties for crimes and treatment dictated for the care of paupers were harsh; laws protecting workers were largely non-existent. So harsh was the temper of the times that Walter Bagehot described the third decade of the nineteenth century and after, the years during which Dickens, of course, was writing, as a time in which 'the unfeeling obtuseness of the early part of the century was to be corrected by an extreme, perhaps excessive, sensibility to human suffering in the years which followed'.[6]

The point is this: if Dickens's intention was to please the Victorian popular audience, he needed to answer to, if not reconcile, all of these conflicting demands. That is, he needed to promote as keen a sensitivity to social injustice and sufferings of the poor as he could – and at the same time entertain with high jinks and high-spirited comedy. He needed to provide as vivid a picture as he could of those sufferings and their causes – and still maintain the reassuring optimism and faith in God and social progress that popular propriety demanded. He needed to provide enough moral rhetoric to 'teach a lesson' – and still be sure that that lesson was neither too radical nor too conservative, and risk losing a part of his audience. And in the midst of satisfying these demands, he needed, as all those of us who have read biographies of Dickens know, to exorcise some of his own private demons – expel some of his own restlessness – as well.

No one, I think, was more suited to reconciling the conflicting demands of the age than was Dickens. He was the quintessential Victorian, who shared all of their contradictions. He was the writer of books crammed full of plot and rhetorical recommendations of family warmth, who confessed that he could never show his affection openly to his own children once they had passed out of infancy. His son, Henry Fielding Dickens's book *Memories of My Father* is most poignant when it speaks to this point. Further, Dickens was a defender of and romanticiser of hearth and home whose own marriage dissolved in a sea of recriminations. He was a protester against prestige and position, who sent his eldest son to Eton (albeit, of course, at the expense of Angela Burdett-Coutts). He was a clear-eyed realist living in the world as it was, whose ironic response to a young writer denouncing that world was 'What a lucky thing it is, you and I don't belong to it.'[7] And he was enough of a romantic to be dismayed and surprised to discover that his first great love Maria Beadnell was at the age of forty-four no longer the charming vixen she had been twenty years before. He was both the urbane and witty after-dinner speaker, and the histrionic actor whose readings moved women to faint and men to cry. He was the incurable optimist and believer in social change whose novels stand as testimony to his faith that human hearts could and did change, and the pessimist who confessed in exasperation to John Forster that he felt 'no faith or hope – not a grain' in either the people or in politics.[8] He was one of those writers who confess that they 'write because [they] can't help it',[9] and yet was also one who could confide quite as readily that he saw himself as 'the modern embodiment of the old Enchanters, whose Familiars tore them to pieces'.[10] He was the calculating businessman and self-disciplined man, who not only made his own fortune, but retrieved his father, his family, colleagues and friends from the edge of financial ruin time and time again, and the restless waif who as his life went on literally drove himself into the grave in a frenzy of work, trying to avoid his own 'giddiness and restlessness of heart', and his own undefined and uncontrollable urges. The proportions changed during his life, of course: he was more restless late in life than he had been earlier; more calculating later in life than he had been earlier; but the contradictions remained with him, both early and late.

He shared the political and social and moral contradictions of his age as well. He saw institutions like the Bowes Academy of William Shaw, where twenty-five boys between the ages of seven and eighteen died and were buried between 1810 and 1834 and another ten went blind from infections left untreated, and saw slums like those of St Giles, Bethnal Green and Saffron Hill where child prostitutes and paupers trudged through the offal and garbage mixed with the mud of the streets – and still believed, if we are to take his novels seriously, that simple, personal goodness of heart and private acts of charity could be the answer to social problems. He wanted to believe he lived in a moral universe in which good was rewarded and evil punished, and yet he wrote novels in which Fate, as often as a just God, determines action and consequence. He saw merit in a democratic social system, and yet he defended the Mechanics' Institute against those who feared it would 'confound the distinctions of society and render people dissatisfied with the grades into which they have fallen' by announcing smugly that 'the different grades of society are so accurately marked, and so very difficult to pass that I have not the slightest fear of any such result'.[11]

There is no shame, of course, in being of several minds about major social issues. As Alexander Welsh shows in his book on Dickens and the city, the city itself was new and complex enough to make such contradictory feelings inevitable: one didn't even know what to do with the mortal remains of all those who died in the cities, since the customary resting places, the parish cemeteries, were finite.[12] Welsh's chapter titles are a litany of the things Victorians felt ambivalent about, and the list is long: work, charity, forgiveness – and the city itself.

In spite of all these contradictions, conflicting impulses, half-formed and contradictory notions about what was and was not to be believed, and what was and was not to be done to make the world a better place; in spite of all of the gaps between what he wanted to be true and what his perceptions told him really was true, Dickens shared, above all, that other characteristic of the Victorians, a constitutional indisposition to expressions of incertitude. Looking for admissions of uncertainty anywhere in Dicken's novels is, as George Bernard Shaw said in another context, like looking for a nautilus in a nursery. Like Mark Tapley, Dickens always needed to 'come out strong'.

My thesis is simple. Dickens reconciled those conflicting demands of his audience, and he satisfied his own conflicting attitudes towards both personal and public issues, simply by parcelling out his intentions and feelings into the variety of modes of presentation he adopts in his novels. Dickens has 'a vision', but that vision is fragmented, so that if one wants to discover how Dickens thinks or feels about anything at all, one must look not only, say, at plot, but at plot and image combined. Not only at character, but at character and rhetoric combined. Indeed, even in something as apparently simple as how Dickens felt about the rising class of men in commerce, Pearl Chester Solomon suggests that Dickens is split in two: 'In part, the question of why Dickens made his good masters fools is inseparable from his fictional technique; from his habit of dividing the attributes of a single person or role amongst several persons. By fragmenting his merchants into their various aspects – in *Nicholas Nickleby* into the grasping Ralph Nickleby and the charitable Cheerybles; in *A Christmas Carol* into the miserly Scrooge, the regenerate Marley and the cherubic Fezziwig – Dickens is able to present both good and bad masters, but he can also avoid having to face his own ambivalence about the master, and his uncertainty about the possibility of any man being at once kindly and commercial.'[13]

The bulk of this study will concern itself with illumination and exemplification of these disharmonies and the meanings I see engendered by them.[14] Since, however, there is no particular reason why the reader should not know immediately what I take those meanings to be, I shall begin with my conclusions. There comes to be in the reader of Dickens's novels, then, a powerful perception of meaning at the point at which the reader begins to see gestural, phrasal, behavioural predictability in Dickens's fictive world run directly up against Dickens's world in description, which turns out to be a world in flux, and always and ever in the process of transformation. Meaning is born at the point at which the reader feels that Dickens's imagic world, a world of grotesque and shape-shifting beasts, is neither being admitted nor acknowledged in the rhetoric of the narrator of the novels. Meaning is born and felt at the point where comic repetition, which Henri Bergson in his essay 'Laughter' calls reassuring because predictable, becomes confused with or is transformed into uncontrolled, unpredictable repetitions which suggest a machine – or a world – gone amuck. Meaning is perceived at the point where the comic meets, and then is often transformed into, the unfunny. An awareness of complex meaning arises at the point at which the reader recognises that the accumulation of detail and description he is being given inhibits rather than facilitates seeing, often at precisely those points at which rhetorically he is being urged to see and perceive. Complexity of meaning as well as of response originates at the point where authorial omniscience and direct rhetorical intervention meet real or assumed authorial bewilderment that evidences itself in the profusion of forms of expression such as *seems, perhaps, if* and *might have been*, forms of language that not only expand the borders of the fictive world in time and in possibility, but also multiply the possibility of what 'truth' might be. When Dickens's own feelings are at war with his public moral pronouncements, we perceive that, for instance, at the same time that rhetorically Dickens is urging an opening of our hearts and homes to the poor, he is constructing a fictive world based on the huddle around the hearth. Thus we feel his message to be both expansive and contractive, inclusive and exclusive, and always both at the same time. One message is offered to us rhetorically, and a conflicting one is embodied in Dickens's plots. To talk only about Dickens's rhetoric, or only about his plots, is to lose this perception of meaning altogether.

We can talk about this kind of meaning in Dickens's novels in formal terms instead. Each of the modes of presentation a writer selects carries with it a set of expectations, and it is out of either the satisfaction or the betrayal of those expectations that meaning in a literary work is generated. What we expect of a picaresque narrative are regular infusions of new and interesting characters. What we don't expect is that those characters will be, as they often are in Dickens's novels, starving paupers and procuresses whose sideline is snipping and selling the hair of young girls. What we expect – what we are led to expect by Dickens rhetorically – is a rational world, clearly described. However, what we get as often as not is a fantastical world in which description, no matter how complete it seems to be, does not always help us 'see' at all. Dickens's rhetorical stance is very often that of the moral admonisher; but his descriptions contradict his faith in the possibility of change. What we expect are mystery stories in which the end brings resolution; what we get often is mystery that exceeds that generated by the plot, and does not go away at the resolution of the plot mystery, or even at the end of the novel. What we expect of a novelist is a reasonable amount of control over form and a consistent point of view. What Dickens provides, as often as not, and perhaps unintentionally, are really two worlds: a world of plot, which is controlled by expectations raised and then satisfied, mystery generated and then solved; and a second world in image and description, which often runs along independent of the world of plot – and sometimes even runs counter to the world of plot. This second world is very often not controlled by form, and has no rhetorical framework or an inadequate rhetorical framework to serve as container and controller of the distressing images (of a city of beasts, for example) that are called up. The effect on us of this not-completely controlled fictive world is a near-approximation of the richness, the complexity and the bewilderment that is a part of life in the very real world, which, of course, is also neither limited nor controlled.

To look carefully at Dickens's modes of description is to see that often great masses of detail are gathered into no coherent pattern at all, and to find that with this unconnected detail we are often forced to make our own connections and our own closures. The reader who reads Dickens is not given a report, but is instead placed in the position of one who has to participate in the initial act of 'seeing'. In the welter of description and detail, some things seem arbitrarily to be left vague, so that perception (as opposed to simply 'seeing') becomes a chancy and a haphazard business – much, of course, as it is in life. Because of Dickens's mode of description, his world in many ways still feels formless, or still seems to be in the process of congealing into a recognisable form. Dickens has an almost compulsive need to describe everything. But real perception involves not seeing everything, but equal parts of seeing and ignoring the irrelevant detail. Whenever and insofar as Dickens doesn't filter out the irrelevant detail, we are not the recipients of Dickens's formed vision so much as we are instead his guests at the gathering of the raw materials for a vision; not passive recipients of a vision so much as we are active participants in the process of its creation.

Oftentimes Dickens's descriptions focus on anything but what is supposedly the centre of his plot action. Some of the most crucial scenes in the novels – the death of Little Nell, for instance – occur off-stage, while our attention is being focused on details elsewhere. Time and time again our attention is split between the scene of the action, where the main characters act and react; and another peripheral world where a whole different set of characters wander quietly into the novels and quietly slip away again, carrying away with them a part of our attention and interest, and often our sympathy as well.

We expect that description will help us see, but often in the novels even this expectation is thwarted, as description and detail are enlisted in an effort to *prevent* our seeing; so that, just as we study the dentist's buttons so we needn't look at the drill, we are sometimes directed to apparently miscellaneous details of setting so that the real vision won't 'hurt' so much. Descriptions in Dickens's novels often become, in other words, a diversionary tactic.

Not only is description responsible for generating complex effects, but so also is the narrator-describer himself. Insofar as that narrator, like the narrator of much of *Oliver Twist*, remains apparently unaffected by the suffering he reports, he creates a reader who surely feels utterly alone in his outrage at the conditions described. Other describers, as we shall see, create equally complex responses.

Repetition is often mentioned as one of Dickens's stylistic 'tics', and we expect it to be used by Dickens as a comic device. Yet repetition can and does work in different ways. In a bewildering world full of objects and people moving unexpectedly in and out of our line of vision, repetitions – of word, phrase, or gesture – can serve as reassuring anchor points; as reassurances that there are some things in the world that are predictable. Thus, some of Dickens's repetitions can be seen as providing security, continuity, assurances that what is, always will be. But it is in the nature of the repetition to suggest the mechanical and the machine-like. And Dickens wrote and lived in a time and for a people who had great fears of a world which seemed to be becoming more and more mechanical. Thus the reassuring phrase or gesture is liable at any moment in Dickens's novels to shade off into the disconcerting realm of the mechanical, suggesting man-becoming-machine. There are worlds of difference between Magwitch's hugging himself in times of stress, a touching and very human repetition, and Flintwinch's periodic grabbing and shaking of Affery, which suggests one of the clattering Victorian machines – a mangle, perhaps – gone mad, or moving with a wilful and unpredictable malevolence. Further, just as the unconscious or natural repetition of phrase or gesture can be charming, can be funny, can even serve to give a character strength and comfort, the conscious or unnatural gesture or repetition we often feel to be – in the case of a Pecksniff or a Bounderby or a Uriah Heep – both unfunny and reprehensible. Dickens's repetitions lie along a continuum, and there is much uncertainty in the reader as to where the line between the reassuring repetition and the disturbing repetition lies. There are a great many characters, from

Mrs Wilfer to Bounderby, from Mr Jellyby to Jaggers, whose repeated gestures and phrases are quite disturbing. Are they to be taken simply as comic repetitions? Or are they muted suggestions of human beings whose patterned-in responses to the world hint that they and their sense no longer receive external stimuli? Or, perhaps most disconcerting of all to Dickens, whose hopes lie in changing human beings and their feelings, did their stock responses suggest a lack of capacity for change, or an inability to change at all? Repetition in Dickens's novels serves not only as a comfort, but at the same time calls up a potential threat.

Part of the complex meaning we feel in Dickens's novels is to be traced to Dickens's particular choices of word or phrase – choices of words that allow for ambiguities or ambivalences by their very nature. There are in the novels, for instance, all those *seemses* and *perhapses*, which serve partly to create and preserve the mystery in Dickens's novels. But oftentimes these same words serve to enrich the novels by providing what might be thought of as 'alternative visions'. Any writer who suggests as Dickens does that conditions are not as good as they might be is almost bound to posit what conditions might be if these conditions were changed. Just as the peripheral world that exists in Dickens's images and description expands the boundaries of his world in space, and as his practice of telescoping time and giving us in his descriptions equal parts of history and prophecy expands the boundaries of his world in time, so his use of the conditional *if* expands his world in possibility as well, signalling social, moral, public, or personal possibilities.

But the *if* can also serve as a refuge for one who cannot or will not take a stand. We all know too well the exasperation that accompanies our hearing someone admit, 'Well, if what you say is true . . .', a phrase which neither affirms nor denies, but provides a safe haven for one who refuses to agree or disagree. Equally exasperating is the advice prefaced by 'If I were you', a phrase that carries with it no responsibility to do what follows, since he who speaks is *not* you. Dickens, like Carlyle, at times takes refuge in precisely these kinds of *ifs*, a habit somewhat surprising and unexpected in a writer who is often otherwise – at least rhetorically – so straightforward. As we shall see, real dilemmas, as well as dilemmas that are real for Dickens but not necessarily so for us (such as the problem of mixed-class marriages) are often similarly couched in the word *if*.

In the same way, *seems* hides a multitude of evasions in the midst of Dickens's rhetorical stance of certainty. Seeming may be false or true, as Dickens's narrator remarks in *Edwin Drood*. The reader of Dickens's novels must in this way, too, become a participant: must, when he encounters the word *seems*, try to separate the *seemses* that are true from those that are not. It is to be expected that a writer of mystery stories will use his share of *seemses*, because they help to generate mystery. But Dickens's often do more and other than this. The reader of Dickens's novels expects to play the game of separating the real thread of the mystery from the false clues and red herrings. He is quite prepared to separate the true *seemses* from the false ones. But what he does not expect, I think, is that there are some *seemses* that will remain unresolved; some that signal a genuine failure or inability to *know* with any certainty. In Dickens's maze of description – of tumbling-down buildings, sizzling meats and scruffy dogs and scruffier people – there is oftentimes buried the phrase 'we saw, or fancied we saw, it makes no difference which', a phrase that thrusts the reader into the peculiar position of trying to determine which is the real and which is not. If at least half the time Dickens intervenes rhetorically with 'My Lords and Gentlemen and Honourable Boards', leaving no doubt where 'truth' lies, the other half of the time the reader confronts prefaces such as 'it may be . . .', 'one may say . . .', 'some said . . . but', or a whole series of *seemses* and *perhapses* that force the reader into the position of trying to sort out from the masses of detail the real from the false, the real from the surreal, or the real from the fantastic or the fairy tale.

Finally, and most importantly, we expect in a novel to learn on its earliest pages how we are to respond to the fictive world being presented. If the literary object doesn't announce its intentions, it *does* announce itself to be a satire or a sermon, a realistic fiction or a lyric poem. But only the foolish reader expects to get through the Dickens world so easily. Because instead, as he opens the pages of each novel (we call them *novels* as a convenience, although Dickens was, as was Melville, wise enough to call them 'books' or 'works' thus avoiding setting up such expectations), the reader must be constantly alert and prepared to shift his expectations or his mode of response as Dickens shifts his mode of presentation. Those critics who, early and late, have talked of Dickens's 'energy of conception' or his 'energy of presentation' are quite right to perceive energy as a large component in the Dickens world. But the great amount of energy that radiates from Dickens's novels is actually in part our own. Reading Dickens, finally, is a participatory sport.

3 Sequence and Consequence: from Truckling Knave to Trickling Blood

> The novel exists . . . as a work of literature only as it is read. As such, it is not a spatial structure of simultaneously related parts but an ever-changing rhythm of relationships.[1]

> By 'meaning' in the novel Dickens clearly has in mind not some abstract moral or maxim, but a complex, enlarging state of consciousness which the novelist dramatises or 'works out' in the course of writing, a vision and interpretation of experience.[2]

Dickens had about as many styles as he had children, and he switched from one style to another – from melodrama to naturalistic description; from rhetorical preachment to comic high-jinks – about as often as he dipped his pen in his inkwell. This is another of those facts about Dickens that we all know well, and yet very seldom do we consider that those shifts from one style to another are themselves responsible for generating some of the meaning the reader of Dickens perceives as he reads. As Seymour Chatman surmises: 'If narrative structure is indeed semiotic – that is, communicates meaning in its own right, over and above the paraphrase-able contents of its story – it should . . . be quadripartite. . . . It should contain (1) a form and substance of expression, and (2) a form and substance of content.'[3] The semiotic import of Dickens's stylistic shifts is, I think, worth some attention, particularly since I suspect that the modern reader of Dickens has become highly sensitised both to the meaning that the ordering of events in a literary text might suggest, and to the meaning that particular stylistic modes of presentation in a text might suggest; has become sensitised to the message-bearing capacities of both form and sequence. Steven Marcus talks about how this happens, in his essay on George Eliot, 'Human Nature, Social Orders, and 19th Century Systems of Explanation':

> A narrative itself sets up in us certain expectations; and in a historical narrative those expectations are raised to a further degree of intensity and certitude. The expectations in question have to do with a temporal series or sequence of events; these units rearrange themselves in an intelligible or coherent order, and by an almost irresistible pressure the temporal sequence of events is conflated with a causal sequence – that is to say a causal (and therefore totally intelligible) structure is made to rise out of a temporal flow that has already been chopped up into distinctive units, almost as if one were to try to demonstrate logically that Venus had to step out of this particular wave rather than the one before or behind it. Furthermore, the historical narrative tends to presuppose a world that has already been constructed, and which, because it seems to have been finished before we make acquaintance with it, gives off its own significance as it is unrolled before us.[4]

One can do all kinds of studies of patterns in Dickens's novels – of symbolic patterns, of imagic patterns; one can talk about all kinds of structures at work in the novels. But structuring and patterning inevitably leaves behind the temporal, step-by-step movement of the novels, and doing that kind of patterning inevitably leaves me feeling quite like I did when my son and I dug up the grave of Fred Paws, an old cat we had buried several years earlier. The experience was not very satisfying. His 'structure' was there all right: we could see how large he had been, could count his teeth and toes, but what we had cared most about in Fred Paws was gone. His patchwork coat, the tail that had curled into a question mark when he was hungry, the shaggy fur were all gone. Standing beside the heap of dirt and bones, I realised that more than another skeletal or structural study of Dickens, we needed to get up close to them; to follow and trace every curve, every sudden or gradual shift from comedy to pathos, from fairy tale to grim reality, from the rise of high moral rhetoric to the descent into bathos, from the chatty descriptions of the urbane, witty observer to the ranting of the hysterical polemicist. Meaning is, of course, something that is primarily an event; something that accumulates as the reader moves through a text, and is generated in large part by the surprises, betrayals, satisfactions, or confusions he experiences as he proceeds through that text. Obviously, since Dickens shifts from rhetor to reporter, from fairy-tale teller to polemicist in the space of a paragraph, an honest and complete reading of even the shortest of Dickens's novels could easily turn out to be interminable. What one can do, though, is provide such a close reading of representative scenes and chapters, tracing carefully the stylistic juxtapositions and shifts, and talking somewhat about at least the characteristic shifts Dickens makes, and the meanings those shifts can be said to generate in readers.

The first chapter of *Dombey and Son*, for instance, might serve as an example. The chapter opens with Dombey seated in a darkened room near his newborn son. What follows is description of the two that is so wry and so fanciful and so inventive that the subject or focus of that description seems to become Dickens or his narrator rather than the characters being described.[5] Newborn Paul Dombey lies in a basket bedstead before the fire 'as if his constitution were analogous to that of a muffin, and it was essential to toast him brown while he was very new' [DS.i.1], and his fists are clenched and curled so that he seems 'to be squaring at existence for having come upon him so unexpectedly' [DS.i.1]. With the delight and sureness of touch of one who is confident he is writing well, Dickens playfully directs our attention first to father, then to son, and back to father again: Father is 'rather bald, rather red'; son is 'very bald, and very red, and somewhat crushed and spotty in his general effect, as yet'. The narrator seems vaguely interested in drawing a moral from what he describes, remarking that

> On the brow of Dombey, Time and his brother Care had set some marks, as on a tree that was to come down in good time — remorseless twins they are for striding through their human forests, notching as they go . . . [DS.i.1],

but that moral is perfunctory at best, and the language in which it is drawn so pleasantly imaginative that it renders the moral quite painless. The reader who reads these opening paragraphs, then, has no reason to expect that he has encountered anything but the comedy of an inventive mind, or to expect that he will be called upon to do anything except laugh and enjoy.

But after the first two paragraphs of this opening chapter, when Dombey begins to speak, we learn that he is not just going to be the object or occasion for laughter. Soon enough, we see him in all of his rigidity, condescending, but only once, to address his dying wife as 'Dear', and we begin to realise that this man is not simply harmlessly comic at all; have intimations that he is in fact largely responsible for her sufferings.

It is a truism of Dickens criticism that Dickens was either not interested in or was not capable of rendering the interior life of his characters. This is patently untrue. In one bold and comprehensive paragraph, Dickens illumines Dombey's interior. How does he feel toward his weak and fading wife? The answer is clear:

> if his wife should sicken and decay, he would be very sorry, and . . . should find a something gone from among his plate and furniture, and other household possessions, which was well worth the having, and could not be lost without sincere regret [DS.i.5].

Consistently and regularly, Dickens intervenes in the narrative of *Dombey and Son* to let us know how Dombey is feeling and thinking – particularly in his relation to Florence, as his indifference changes to discomfort, his discomfort to jealousy, and his jealousy to a 'positive hatred', as Dickens tells John Forster in the famous letter of 25 July 1846, in which Dickens describes at length his plans for *Dombey and Son*. After Dombey's character is delineated, described, demonstrated, exposed and disposed of in the space of a few paragraphs, Dickens returns to his comic mode, introducing Dombey's sister Mrs Chick, who bursts on to the pages of the novel 'dressed in a very juvenile manner, particularly as to the tightness of her bodice' [DS.i.5]. Next, with that quintessentially Dickensian touch, comedy and tragedy are merged. Mrs Dombey is dying upstairs, says Mrs Chick, because she won't 'make an effort' [DS.i.6].

From this point until the end of the first chapter the reader feels the tension between the comedy and the impending tragedy building, the comedy trying to maintain its ascendancy, and the tragedy impinging with ever-increasing urgency and frequency. Downstairs in the drawing room is Miss Tox in her sartorial disarray, 'carrying about small bags with snaps to them, that went off like little pistols when they were shut up' [DS.i.7]. Upstairs in the bedroom Mrs Dombey prepares to die. To read this chapter with the sensitivity it deserves is to feel that both Dickens and his readers are trying desperately to cling to the comic, while the tragic impinges with an urgency that cannot be denied, just as the watches of the physicians at Mrs Dombey's bedside seem to tick with an ever-increasing loudness, announcing time and mortality that will not be denied. The comic makes one last valiant effort to reassert its dominance: Mrs Chick leans over the bed to demand that Mrs Dombey 'make an effort'. But in the end Mrs Dombey dies, and the scene and the chapter that had begun as high-spirited comedy ends as a tragedy in which the weak-willed Mrs Dombey, her spirit broken by her proud husband, dies, and the figurative, funny muffin toasting before the fire becomes a real-life motherless child.

This progression from exuberant high-spirited comedy to real-life tragedy is a common one in Dickens's novels, and depending upon whether the one or the other asserts primacy in the reader's memory, one feels Dickens to be either a 'dark' or a 'comic' writer. The psychological composition of each of us that would dictate who of us would remember the one and who the other is beyond anyone's ken. One can, however, say something about the intentions and psychology of a writer who continually wrote in such a way. Both John Forster and Edgar Johnson in their biographies of Dickens note that his solution to his own dissatisfactions, restlessnesses and personal tragedies was to try to escape them temporarily by indulging in comic high-jinks. Any real discomfort, from fleas in his beds when he stayed in a hotel in Lausanne, Switzerland, to the largeness of his family, could be relieved if not dispelled if only it could be exuberantly blown up into a joke. With his own progeny appearing with alarming frequency (he was to father ten children), he masked and relieved his own distress with comedy:

> What strange kings those were in the Fairy times, who, with three thousand wives and four thousand seven hundred and fifty concubines found it necessary to offer up prayers in all the Temples for a prince as beautiful as the day! I have some idea, with only one wife and nothing particular in any other direction, of interceding with the Bishop of London to have a little service in Saint Paul's beseeching that I may be considered to have done enough towards my country's population.[6]

Unsatisfied early in his marriage with his wife Catherine, whose somewhat quiet nature was no match for his own high-spirited one,

Dickens relieved his dissatisfactions by pretending to be in love with Queen Victoria, and crushed by her marriage to Prince Albert. For a full month, Dickens wrote letters to his friends, telling how he paced outside her bedroom window the evening of her marriage, and 'lay down in the mud of the Long Walk, and refused all comfort'.[7] Threatening to kill himself, he announced that he

> should wish to be embalmed and to be kept (if practicable) on the top of the triumphal arch at Buckingham Palace when she was in town, and on the northwest turret of the Round Tower when she is at Windsor.[8]

He would portray life as it is – in all its dissatisfactions and all its uglinesses, even unto dealth – but he would also provide the antidote to dissatisfaction that worked for him. This is why it comes to be that Dickens moves with such regularity and rapidity from the comic to the tragic and back again.

This is not, of course, the only sequence of modes of presentation that Dickens uses, and other kinds of sequences generate different meanings. Chapter xxxi of *Dombey and Son*, in which Dombey and Edith Granger are wed, is quite different, though no less rich. It begins with what R. P. Blackmur calls 'putative description',[9] or the kind of description one can find in Herman Melville's *Pierre*, the kind of description 'that cannot contribute any material of emotion beyond that which may be contained in a stock exclamation'.[10] Like Melville, Dickens begins by personifying nature in a most standard way:

> Dawn, with its passionless blank face, steals shivering to the church beneath which lies the dust of little Paul and his mother, and looks in at the windows. It is cold and dark. Night crouches yet, upon the pavement, and broods, sombre and heavy, in nooks and corners of the building . . . dawn moans and weeps for its short reign, and its tears trickle on the window-glass, and the trees against the churchwall bow their heads, and wring their many hands in sympathy [DS.xxxi.436].

It doesn't seem either too harsh or too inaccurate to say that in this passage Dickens is inspiring no more than a stock response from his readers. Since no scene has yet been played out, such revving up of the rhetorical engines must be regarded as a kind of attempt to make the reader pay in advance: to care about those weeping windows before we know anything about why they weep. There are two ways in which a reader might respond to this style and mode of presentation: reject it and find it false – since how *could* one respond sensitively to a scene not yet played out; or simply understand that what is being proferred is a kind of invitation to emotional game-playing, relax, and enjoy the pleasure of pretending to feel emotions.

The latter course seems to be the one that most readers who encounter this opening scene would choose, particularly in light of the fact that soon enough the reader is to encounter its replacement: a mode that resembles nothing so much as that of the fairy tale. It is to be recognised largely by and in Dickens's word-order and diction: 'And now comes bright day,' says the narrator in the second paragraph of this chapter, and 'A vinegary face has Mrs Miff, and a mortified bonnet, and eke a thirsty soul for sixpences and shillings.' [DS. xxxi.436]. Just as Dickens's putative description that opened this chapter, his fairy tale narrative confirms the fact that readers are to relax and enjoy, precisely as do the underlings and hirelings of Mr Dombey's household are described as enjoying the preparations for the wedding, quite oblivious to any serious concerns.

A wedding is to take place, and it is a wedding that in more ways than one will have serious consequences for Dombey himself, for Edith, for Florence, for, in brief, the novel. But instead of getting to work describing that wedding, Dickens first generates that putative description, then turns to fairy-tale diction, and finally introduces his readers to dozens of peripheral characters who do the exact opposite of focusing attention either on that wedding, or on the presumed importance of that wedding. Such a progression in the narrative must suggest one of several things to the reader: (1) that the wedding cannot even hold the attention of its creator, who is fascinated enough by peripheral characters to be unable to resist describing them in detail; (2) that, because of the way Dickens is presenting his material, this event is not to be taken seriously, and, for that matter, by extension, neither is the plot in general, except as an occasion and an excuse for comedy or fairy-tale description; (3) that Dickens's attention to this peripheral world creates a vision of experience which in its turn suggests that the world outside the boundaries of the plot is large, and as full of action, drama and problems as the world that is presumably at the centre of his stage. Dickens's modes of presentation tell us, in other words, that to focus attention is to arbitrarily choose from among the multitude of possibilities that exist in the real world; to focus is to shut out.

To look more closely at the style in which these peripheral characters are conveyed is to learn something else. The style itself reproduces the 'stir and bustle' which it talks about. The length of sentences gradually increases, largely as a result of coordinating conjunctions and semicolons, all of which, of course, serve to connect events one with another, but without expressing anything like a causal relationship of one thing to another. This might be said to be the kind of style that might well be used by a reporter who finds things happening too fast for him to do other than say exactly what Dickens's narrator says: 'Mr Towlinson is an object of greater consideration than usual to the housemaid, and the cook says at breakfast-time that one wedding makes many, which the housemaid can't believe, and don't think true at all' [DS.xxxi.437]. Such a sentence provides a sharp contrast to the crafted, conscious, highly artificed sentences and style that opened this chapter. The first suggest a craftsman conscious of the language he is using more so than the events that language describe; the work of a craftsman *creating* a 'reality'. The second suggest a harried reporter trying only to report a reality that already exists.

The two modes of presentation that open this wedding chapter, then, are very clearly different, even though both would fall under the general heading of 'descriptive' modes. But furthermore, because they are sequential – because they follow one another – other meanings are generated by them as well. The sensitive reader is bound to feel that he has encountered a writer who is at the start very consciously in control of both his language and the reality he creates and describes, but who gradually finds himself in the thick of the scene he describes. Things begin to happen too fast for him to control, and reality – and not artifice – takes over. Dickens's modal sequence might suggest something else: since the artificed sentences are all about nature, and the breathless reporting comes with the introduction of people on the stage, one might presume that it is the very complexity and busy-ness of human beings that overwhelms the power of the narrator to control them in language. Because of these two modes of presentation following one another, the reader feels both the confusions and complexities of human beings in the universe, and the, by contrast, artfulness and perhaps artificiality of the carefully wrought description that precedes that confusion.

But I am not naïve. I am in no way suggesting that Dickens's narrative 'really' got out of his control. Of course, the breathless, harried description of peripheral characters is quite as much a conscious artifice as the putative description of nature that precedes it. Both modes are without a doubt the creation of a writer who thrived on contrasts; who jumped in a window at a friend's house to dance a frenzied hornpipe, only to leap out again and appear at the front door a moment later as the staid and respectable guest.[11]

Dombey, of course, wants his wedding taken seriously. He is, as a matter of fact, upset with Major Bagstock's joking about his mother-in-law-to-be. But Dickens is on the side of those who would laugh, and for a page or two more, the wedding preliminaries become the occasion for laughter. But that comic mode lasts only for one last paragraph, and it ends with Edith Granger's appearance on the scene. At this point, the mode becomes something like that of the sensation novel. If Edith doesn't here have a 'heaving bosom', as she does elsewhere, she certainly does have that 'disdainful and defiant figure, standing there, composed, erect, inscrutable of will, resplendent and majestic in the zenith of its charms, yet beating down, and treading on, the admiration that it challenges' [DS.xxxi.442]. I cannot speak for other readers, but at this point I, at least, am puzzled. I presume that Dickens wants me to take Edith seriously, and yet the mode in which she is presented is so much that of sensation novelists, or of melodrama, that a 'real' response seems somehow inappropriate. For a brief moment the scene does become real, as Edith struggles with her mother, insisting that Florence not come under the influence of Mrs Skewton, as Edith had done. It is almost as if the reader's perception of the real psychosexual, socioeconomic import of Edith's plight grows in spite of – rather than because of – the narrator, who seems to want to go on being comic, melodramatic, or to do anything rather than take his material seriously.

Perhaps this happens because, as was always the case, Dickens wanted to present potentially painful material only after, as he said, 'throwing comicality over it.'[12] While he was composing *Nicholas Nickleby*, he thought 'the rascalities of the Yorkshire schoolmasters were so severe that in revealing them he had to keep down the strong truth and [throw] as much comicality over it as [he] could, rather than disgust the reader with its fouler aspects.'[13] At points in *The Uncommercial Traveller*, he suggests much the same thing.[14] Knowing what we do of Dickens's experience with marriage – his own and his brother Fred's to Miss Thompson – perhaps marriage itself was a subject that needed comicality thrown over it to make it palatable.

The shifts in mode of presentation during the wedding chapter go on, and I leave my readers to decide what those shifts do. At the end of the scene, however, Dickens carefully describes the reactions of all of those who have witnessed it. And their reactions, I would say, are exactly as multitudinous and as various as the reactions that Dickens's modes of presentation have generated in his readers. Miss Tox emerges 'wounded, but not exasperated' [DS.xxxi.445]. Captain Cuttle emerges 'much improved by his religious exercises, . . . and in a peaceful frame of mind' [DS.xxxi.445]. Mr Toots leaves church 'in torments of love', while his friend The Chicken imagines ways of 'doubling up Mr Dombey'. Mrs Perch nearly faints; Sownds the Beadle and Mrs Miff sit upon the steps to count the change they have gained by the affair; the sexton 'tolls a funeral'. Here Dickens seems to be describing what he obviously believes to be true. One event – a wedding, for instance – can and does generate varied responses in all who see it. So also, the scene of the wedding is responsible, because of the modes in which Dickens renders it, for generating an equivalent number of responses in those who read it. The subject of this short segment of Dickens's novel becomes, then, not only the wedding of Dombey and Edith, but an introduction to all of the responses it is possible to have to a wedding like that of Dombey and Edith.

In truth, Dickens's shifts in mode of presentation might be said to be doing that primarily all of the time. They are exercises in response; practice in laughter and tears, and more than that, practice in rapid alternation from one to the other. As London winds up for the Gordon Riots in *Barnaby Rudge*, for instance, the reader must feel constant dis-ease at a world that seems to be behaving melodramatically. ('Whir-r-r,' says Sim Tappertit. 'Something may come of this. I hope it mayn't be human gore. Whir-r-r' [BR.iv.39].) But in that melodramatic response to life lie the seeds for very real violence. Opposing factions shout melo-dramatic imprecations at each other in the streets. Haredale calls Gashford a 'servile, False, and truckling knave' [BR.xliii.330]. But in the space of a minute the tone and mood of this scene change, and the melodrama becomes real drama. Someone in the crowd hurls a rock at Haredale, and the narrator reports that 'the blood sprung freely from the wound, and trickled down his coat' [BR.xliii.331]. From truckling knave to trickling blood is always a very short jump in Dickens's world, and just at the point when the reader might feel that he is free to lapse into a self-indulgent or sentimental response to Dickens's melodrama, that melodrama is transformed into something quite serious, and to which a sentimental or melodramatic response is neither appropriate nor sufficient. As we shall see in a later chapter, Dickens's modes of description reveal him to be one who saw the world as a place very much in the process of transforming before his eyes. The transforming world – which was one moment harmless and charming, and the next threatening – demanded alertness, demanded a readiness to alter one's expectations of and response to that world. And Dickens's style, which is so frequently shifting from one mode of presentation to another, places precisely the same demands upon its readers. John Ruskin once said that a man of very strong feeling will necessarily be a poor judge of art because he will be likely to see a thunderstorm in a paint smudge. But it must also be true that a man of weak feeling will be a poor judge of art because he will lack the sensitivity to detect all that works of art *suggest*, rather than merely state. Dickens's multiple modes of presentation suggest much more than his plots, themes, images and rhetoric state.

Having established the principle that the effect of any element of Dickens's style must be seen as being dependent upon the other elements present with it, and that sequence and context illumine intention and determine the effect of particular modal or stylistic choices, I should like to devote the remainder of my study to elucidating what I believe to be the shifts or juxtapositions, and sometimes cohabitations, of mode and style most frequently present in Dickens's novels, and consequently most responsible for generating the reader's responses to the Dickens world.

4 The Reader at Work

I THE RHETORICS OF IMAGE AND IDEA

> The role of the reader is not to use the commentary as a key to the narrative so much as it is to interpret the commentary in relation to the narrative and the narrative in relation to the commentary, with a view to achieving a formulation of this relationship which respects its hierarchical structure while relativising the commentary in relation to the textual whole.[1]

> As the imagery would be a translation of the idea into sensory terms, criticism might conversely propose to retranslate this sensory version back into purely dialectical or ideological terms.[2]

The rather opaque suggestion with which I begin this chapter, a quotation from Ross Chambers's 'Commentary in Literary Texts', really offers a very sensible and fruitful way to go about talking about what literary texts mean. Ordinarily, critics distinguish between *histoire* (the story or narrative), and *discours* (commentary of the narrator).[3] This usual distinction, however, fails to take into account one crucial fact: elements of that *histoire*, or story, may be serving also the function of commentary. Professor Chambers reminds us in his article that there is always operative in criticism a sort of situation of 'privilege', in which the reader always decides to give 'greater significance to one structural pattern over some other, perhaps equally valid mode of analysis or reading'.[4] In this chapter, I should like to suggest that Dickens's images indeed serve not merely as parts of his *histoire*, or narrative, but are very much a part of his implicit commentary as well.

There is, of course, a wealth of explicit commentary in Dickens's novels, as we all know. Charles Dickens first entered the gallery as a court reporter at the early age of nineteen, writing for the *True Sun*. At twenty-three he became a reporter for the *Morning Chronicle*.

Sitting hour after hour, day after day, in Doctors' Commons, the young Dickens must have received not only an aural, but a tactile sense of the rhetoric of advocacy, as he recorded in the shorthand he had learned from his uncle Barrows the proceedings of the Court. When he began to write novels, it is probably not surprising that that same rhetoric of advocacy passed through his pen on to the pages of his fictions, so much so that the energy that propels them forward remains rhetorical and polemical to the end, even, as we shall see, when that mode was to all intents and purposes irrelevant or inappropriate to the story being told. So that we might better understand the Dickens world and our own responses to it, however, I should like to restore this polemical rhetoric to Dickens's descriptions and his moral admonitions to his plot actions. Where, precisely, can we expect to find those rhetorical flights and moral admonitions that we tend to pass over as we read? When they occur, how do they alter our perception of and reaction to the scenes in which they are found? And most important of all, what is the *relation*, in specific passages, between Dickens's rhetoric and his plots; between the world of image and the world of rhetoric?

In the opening scenes of *Little Dorrit*, Dickens, as is his almost invariable practice, carefully establishes the tone of his story. Dickens, or his narrator, is at great pains to create images of Rigaud and Cavalletto as birds and/or as beasts. In their prison cell, Rigaud's eyes are 'sharp rather than bright', and they 'glitter'. He is said to have a 'hook nose' and eyes too close together 'to suggest the king of beasts' [LD.I.i.3]. John Cavalletto's hands are 'scaled and knotted' [LD.I.i.5], suggesting the claws of a bird more than the hands of a man. When the jailer brings his young daughter to show her 'her father's birds' [LD.I.i.4], what we have been given in image and metaphor finally becomes explicit: the prisoners really are birds. When shortly thereafter Rigaud is released from prison, Cavalletto is said to look 'like a lower animal – like some impatient ape, or roused bear of the smaller species' [LD.I.i.13]. 'Like a caged animal' he 'leaps nimbly down, runs round the chamber, leaps nimbly up again, clasps the grate and tries to shake it' [LD.I.i.13]. H. P. Sucksmith's account of Dickens's manuscript at this point reveals that Dickens is consciously increasing the bird imagery in this passage, even at proof stage:

> The other [man] BIRD remained as before, except for an impatient glance at the basket . . . .We must break it to get it

through INTO THE CAGE. So, there's a [good] TAME bird, to kiss the little hand.[5]

In the succeeding chapter, the references to people as beasts and birds continue. Mr Meagles grumbles that the French are a people 'always howling' [LD.I.ii.15]. Shortly thereafter the reader meets Mr Meagles's daughter (whose nickname, of course, is Pet), and then to Tattycoram, who soon enough in one of her many fits of exasperation, or failures to 'count one and twenty', calls the Meagles family 'Brutes! Beasts! Devils! Wretches!' [LD.I.ii.26]

One might say that Dickens had a bit of a problem with imagic consistency here. Cavalletto can't be both a bird and 'an impatient ape or roused bear of the smaller species' any more than Rigaud can be both a bird with hook nose and glittering eyes, and at the same time 'the king of beasts'. However, it may be that Dickens's apparently confused images are explicable as a kind of *discordia concors* of the kind Samuel Johnson talks about in his *Lives of the English Poets*; a combination of dissimilar images intended to promote a new perception altogether. In this event, the reader would come to understand that Dickens's vision is one not only of a world full of beasts, birds, devils, wretches and demons, but a world in which those very beasts and birds tend, from one moment to the next, to change shape and form before our eyes. If image has the function of providing implicit commentary, then there is no doubt here about what that commentary is.

But look at how, rhetorically, Dickens ends this same scene. Here is the concluding paragraph of the first chapter, the paragraph which sums up what we have just seen in image:

And thus, ever by day and night, under the sun and under the stars, climbing the dusty hills and toiling along the weary plains, journeying by land and journeying by sea, coming and going so strangely, to meet and to act and react to one another, move all we restless travellers through the pilgrimage of life [LD.I.ii.27].

This strikes me as a curious summation of the scene itself. Nowhere in the rhetoric is there any acknowledgement at all of the strange vulture-like birds, or of the howling people, or of the man who paces his cage and climbs the bars of his cell like an animal. Instead we are told that we have just seen 'restless travellers through the pilgrimage of life'. Furthermore, we are told that this is what we have seen in prose that, because of the balanced sentences, has a rhythmic, even soothing, cadence.

What we have here is a classic example of what Wayne Booth calls a 'particular kind of disharmony between idea and dramatised object'.[6] Ross Chambers envisions three main 'registers' of writing: narrative, description and commentary. He assumes that the 'solidarity of narration and description justifies their being grouped together or constituting the "topic" of literary discourse', with the function of commentary being to 'correlate the narrative and/or descriptive text with a context'.[7] These categories are fine and helpful, but I am not so sure that Professor Chambers anticipated that at times the commentary provided by the images used in description would sabotage any 'solidarity' between narration and description. Surely our response to Dickens's world on such an occasion as this must be extremely complex? For who are we to believe? The narrator, who has just conjured up a scene of beasts, birds, caged animals, howling people and demons? Or Dickens, or his rhetorical intervenor, who enters with such a comfortable and comforting message. Dickens's main characters may be as as naïve and sweet as Pet, and as charming as Mr Meagles, and his rhetorical tone may be one that assures us of an essential order and reason in the universe, but how do we make ourselves forget that Dickens, or his narrator, has just told us that the people of London are 'living in fifty-thousand lairs' [LD.I.iii.28]? The answer, I think, is that we don't; that we carry away from his novel both images, and both visions of the world at the same time. It is futile to speculate on whether Dickens was or was not aware of how much more and other he had created in his world of image than he acknowledges in his rhetoric; whether he really believed that some assurances about 'restless travellers' could dispel the demons he had just invoked. Regardless, the scene itself, in the vividness of its detail, simply bursts the bounds of its creator's rhetoric, and once created seems to run on out of Dickens's rhetorical control.

It is commonly recognised that one of the purposes of artistic form is to act as a kind of controller of the vision presented by the artist. Form walls off that vision from our own experience, enclosing any potentially discomfiting information in a framework that assures the reader that what he is encountering is 'art', and not real, and therefore poses no threat, and demands no real action. John Crowe Ransom suggests, for instance, that metre in poetry may serve as such a kind of 'false security', giving us the illusion of control and order. It lulls us so that the poet may say whatever he wishes, and still we feel no threat, 'for so long as the poet appears to be working faithfully at his metrical engine'.[8] Steven Marcus suggests that narrative itself 'offers assurances to its society of readers because the world it represents has already been defined and in some sense closed off; things in it, in other words, *have already happened*'.[9]

If poetic metre and prose narrative can both be thought of as means of 'controlling' and reassuring readers, rhetoric itself must also be seen as a kind of framework or 'container' that has as its function an attempt to assure us that the beasts and demons evoked in image are controlled; are conscious creations of the artist. Simon Lesser, in a particularly appropriate analogy, likens the artist to 'an animal trainer. We feel safe,' he says, 'no matter how fearful the animals brought out.'[10] But Dickens is finally not a very good animal trainer. In truth, as above, there are times at which he quite ignores the wild beasts he calls up, so the reader is left to fight them off as best he can himself.

One must hasten to acknowledge, of course, that ideas or rhetoric, even at their strongest, can, in fact, never 'contain' images. As John Crowe Ransom suggests,

[image] cannot be dispossessed of a primordial freshness, which idea can never claim. An idea is derivative and tamed. The image is in the natural or wild state, and it has to be discovered there, not put there, obeying its own law and none of ours. We think we can lay hold of image and take it captive, but the docile captive is not the real image, but the idea, which is the image with its character beaten out of it.[11]

As we know from Dickens's account of how he wrote (mostly in letters he wrote to friends), he may have begun with an idea, but in the heat of creative fury it was image that propelled him on. And insofar as Dickens's images were not contrived to illustrate some idea; are instead in what Ransom calls 'the natural or wild state', and insofar as those images go by unimpeded by ideas or rhetoric, or only insufficiently commented upon and contained by rhetoric, they are not only that much more powerful, but that much more threatening as well.

I needn't add, I think, that it is not only *Little Dorrit*, but all of Dickens's novels, that have that world in image in which humans are beastlike. And in none of them are those images acknowledged with any thoroughness. Most critics say that Dickens's novels are to some extent written from a child's point of view, and to the child, the world really may seem and feel as though it is inhabited by beasts that slouch and birds that swoop. But the imagic world in Dickens's novels does more and other than simply harken back to the world of our childhood. In fact, I would propose that there is not really, as the title of Humphrey House's book suggested, *The Dickens World*, but there are really *two* worlds. One is the world of the plot and plot action. It is the world in which, for instance, the 'mystery' of Pip's great expectations and his unexpected benefactor's re-velation are played out. It is also the world of 'moral', in which Dickens shows and tells us rhetorically what pride can do to a sensitive and worthy young boy and how humility can and will be rewarded, as Pip's ultimately is.[12] But there is a second world, entirely the product of the constant flow of images in the novel, where Magwitch is 'a eel', who eats 'very like a dog', where Pumblechook has a 'mouth like a fish', where Pip being lectured feels like 'an unfortunate little bull in a Spanish arena . . . smartingly touched up by moral goads', and where Mrs Joe 'pounces on Pip like an eagle on a lamb', and gets him ready for his first visit to Miss Havisham by bathing him, and then 'trussing him up' much like a fowl for roasting. Although these images are called up in metaphors which presumably are meant to carry forward the plot action, in fact they often seem to accumulate in such a way that they create an entirely separate and separable world that exists alongside of, and independent of, the world of plot. This beastlike world is a world of real mystery rather than contrived plot mystery. It is a world where strange beasts of mysterious shape and origin leap and lunge at us – as they leap and lunge at Pip – without forewarning. And it is in this figurative rendering of the experience of living at least as much as it is in the mechanical working out of plot, that Dickens's power and his vision lie. Unlike what happens in the world of plot, the mystery in the world of image does not and cannot end in 'resolution'. How the world gets to be peopled by beasts and demons is a mystery that is never solved. For some, like Geoffrey Tillotson, there is mystery even in the fact of those imagic descriptions themselves:

> Are Dickens's descriptions no more than a silent criticism of the inadequacy of the seeing and observing done by most of us, and no more than an indication that Dickens's bodily apparatus was a

more efficient one than our own? Or did his superiority lie in what the mind added to the report supplied to it by the bodily apparatus?[13]

Is the world really so bad, or is my sensibility deficient, that I can't see that beastly world without Dickens's help. The reader finds no help in answering those questions, or solving those mysteries, in Dickens's commentary.

Simon Lesser makes an interesting observation about the way we read fiction, and about the way in which we react to images as we encounter them. In largest part, he suggests the images we encounter in fiction register on our minds *as images*:

> The images are often too thick with meaning and they succeed one another too rapidly to be anatomised. This is obviously the case when we watch a motion picture or a play, but the situation is not so very different when we read fiction: our desire to learn what happens next, to take in the entire story, reinforces our natural tendency to depend upon our immediate, intuitive understanding.[14]

Three things, he says, combine so as to oppose conceptualisation when we read: curiosity (or the rush to see what happens next); the desire to avoid unnecessary effort (by reading slowly and conceptualising each image as it passes by); and censorship (of the superego trying to spare us pain). As a result, we formulate no more than a small part of what we *understand* when we read fiction. Further, we are particularly unlikely to formulate perceptions that would arouse anxiety if we were to make them more explicit.[15] Lesser is here, as is his usual case, making a case for the way he thinks we censor what is psychologically embarrassing to us. But the dynamics he describes operate for other reasons. Because of Dickens's mystery plots, the reader's conscious attention and rational faculties are focused on the world of plot, trying to 'see what happens next'; trying to find clues and to solve mysteries. Because of Dickens's moral rhetoric, we feel, with a part of our selves, assured of a world responsive to goodness and reason. But at the same time we are absorbing – almost unconsciously – an endless series of images, the *rhetorical* nature of which and the message of which is that the world is, quite literally, a beastly place. From one point of view, Dickens's mystery plots and his moral rhetoric might both be seen as a kind of diversion that serves to protect us from that vision of society that suggests that we live in a society of beasts.

Interestingly enough, this parallel world created by Dickens's images seems to function in two quite opposite ways. The rational reader in all of us, confronting this fantastical world in image, is assured that this world is indeed fantastical and not real, and certainly not at all threatening. As Norman Holland suggests, it is our conscious knowledge that we are dealing with 'unreality' that allows us to relax and enjoy the fictional world.[16] But in the end, the very accumulation of those images tends somehow to materialise our own inner fears. The city really is frightening, and really is inhabited – in our imagination and surely in the imagination of Dickens – by strange and wild beasts who are not to be trusted. Dickens's images are, then, much like his repetitions, as we shall see in a later chapter,[17] creative of both reassurance and danger at the same time. The Dickens world is one moment all people, the next moment all beasts, and yet another moment people confronting beasts, and it is constantly changing shape and form, from one to the other and back again. By juxtaposing rational rhetoric and images embodying irrational fears, Dickens manages to recreate the experience of living in the London of the nineteenth century, a London which was itself very much in the process of changing shape and form.

All of his life Dickens tried to modify the impulse toward insistent rhetoric that he had acquired early in his career as a journalist and shorthand writer. If he couldn't or didn't want entirely to substitute 'the bland smile of the periodical essay for the glare of the propagandist',[18] he could at least integrate his insistent rhetoric with his images and his plots, and this is what he tried to do. But surely as late as *Our Mutual Friend* he had not managed to do so. *Our Mutual Friend* is full of neat rhetorical pronouncements: on the evils of Podsnappery, on the goodness of many people of the lower classes like Betty Higden; on the nature of the criminal [OMF.III.ix.546]; and even on the advisability of setting up better grave markings at the graves of the poor so they can be more easily found by relatives of people buried there [OMF.III.ix.515]. Dickens tries to turn even the Boffins into an occasion for rhetoric or moral:

> These two ignorant and unpolished people had guided themselves so far on in their journey of life, by a religious sense of duty and desire to do right. Ten thousand weaknesses and absurdities

might have been detected in the breasts of both; ten thousand vanities additional, possibly, in the breast of the woman. But the hard wrathful and sordid nature that had wrung as much work out of them as could be got in their best days, for as little money as could be paid to hurry on their worst, had never been so warped but that it knew their moral straightness and respected it. In its own despite, in a constant conflict with itself and them, it had done so. And this is the eternal law. For evil often stops short at itself and dies with the doer of it. But good, never! [OMF.I.ix.101]

In spite of this kind of strongly moral rhetoric that tries to contain, justify and explain *Our Mutual Friend*, what lingers in our memory is not that world of moral rhetoric so much as the world in image, where Gaffer Hexam is 'half savage', and is 'a roused bird of prey'. If men would treat Betty Higden and her kind better, be less susceptible to Podsnappery and the brushing away of suffering with a sweep of the hand, everyone would be happier, and all would be well. At war with this rational and moral conception of the universe is Dickens's own imagic perceptions of what life felt like in the city. A city of beasts can hardly be expected to be responsive to our Christian assumptions. What Barbara Hardy says of *Bleak House* can fairly be said of all of Dickens's novels, and for the same reason. Its 'conclusion is only partially responsive to the rest of the novel, [and] squeezes its solace through too narrow an exit'.[19]

2 RHETORIC AND PLOT

Dickens could perfectly well dissolve what he wanted to communicate into dialogue and action. . . . but he seems unable to trust to that alone, or else, he cannot control altogether his indignation at some monstrous feature of the life of his time.[1]

When Esther Summerson visits a bricklayer's hovel and sees how the two women there love and care for one another and share one another's miseries she is quite touched, and confesses

I thought it very touching to see these two women, coarse and shabby and beaten, so united; to see what they could be to one another; how the heart of each to each was softened by the hard trials of their lives. I think the best side of such people is almost hidden from us: What the poor are to the poor is little known, excepting to themselves and God [BH.viii.109].

This is heavily moralistic prose, and also one of the many occasions Dickens devises so that he might introduce his Victorian readers to what he once called 'the soul of goodness in humble things'. But on this occasion, it seems perfectly appropriate and unobjectionable rhetoric, and it is such because it is prompted directly by the action in the novel at this point, and because the person who speaks these words is a character in that action and not Dickens intervening *in propria persona.*

But this rhetoric, in its restraint and in the fact that it grows out of a specific situation in the plot, is really rather atypical. More typical is this passage from *Martin Chuzzlewit.* When young Martin lounges about London jobless and aimless, pawning his watch and clothes to buy his bread, he becomes more and more unabashedly indolent. At this point in the narrative Dickens's narrator goes on a bit of a rhetorical flight:

Oh moralists, who treat of happiness and self-respect, innate in every sphere of life, and shedding light on every grain of dust in God's highway, so smooth below your carriage wheels, so rough beneath the tread of naked feet, bethink yourselves in looking on the swift descent of men who *have* lived in their own esteem, that there are scores of thousands breathing now, and breathing thick with painful toil, who in that high respect have never lived at all, nor had a chance of life! Go ye, who rest so placidly upon the Sacred Bard who had been young, and when he strung his harp was old, and had never seen the righteous forsaken, or his seed begging their bread; go Teachers of content and honest pride, into the mine, the mill, the forge, the squalid depths of deepest ignorance, and uttermost abyss of man's neglect, and say can any hopeful plant spring up in air so foul that it extinguishes the soul's bright torch as fast as it is kindled! And, oh! ye Pharisees of the nineteenth hundredth year of Christian knowledge, who sound-ingly appeal to human nature, see first that it be human. Take heed it has not been transformed, during your slumber and the sleep of generations, into the nature of the Beasts [MC.xiii.224].

This is the kind of rhetoric the Leavises say Victorian readers loved, being 'avid listeners to and purchasers of sermons'.[2] But it is also the kind of rhetoric, if we be honest, we admit we tend to pass over in silence when we build interpretations of Dickens's novels. But those passages are there, and they must play their part in generating a part of the meaning Dickens's novels have. According to Seymour Chatman, a narrative structure contains two kinds of statements: what he calls 'process' statements, and 'stasis' statements. A 'process' statement is any description of plot actions; of events. A 'stasis' statement is a direct statement to the reader: 'He had no friends' is a 'stasis' statement.[3] Dickens's novels are full of 'stasis' statements that contradict his 'process' statements. It may be perfectly true that 'moralists' have a 'smooth path below their carriage wheels', and those who have 'naked feet' find the dust 'rough', but what has this statement to do with young Martin Chuzzlewit – who is hardly in danger of having naked feet?

Just as there are often disharmonies between Dickens's images and his rhetoric, there are, then, disharmonies between his plot action and his rhetoric; points at which Dickens suddenly wrests the centre stage from his characters to announce the moral to be drawn from his scene. If in the earlier case there is not a powerful enough rhetoric to contain the threats that image pose, in such cases as this quite the opposite occurs. It is this phenomenon, no doubt, that prompted F. R. Leavis to remark that intention is often very insistent in Dickens, without its being taken up in any inclusive way that informs and organises a coherent whole.[4] In the passage above, who is the audience to whom that rhetoric is addressed? What, specifically, has it to do with Martin Chuzzlewit? Who are the 'Pharisees'? And whoever Dickens's audience was meant to be, what would Dickens have them do?

As Little Dorrit walks through Covent Garden, Dickens turns this occasion into another chance to admonish his readers in the middle of a passage of description:

> . . . having all those arches in it, where the miserable children in rags among whom she had just now passed, like young rats, slunk and hid, fed on offal, huddled together for warmth, and were hunted about (look to the rats young and old, ye Barnacles, for before God they are eating away our foundations, and will bring the roof on our heads!) [LD.I.xiv.166]

Here in a rhetorical parenthesis is an admonition in the most urgent terms. Yet the reader might be said to be a bit puzzled. He had been following Amy Dorrit through the streets of London. He had not expected such an outburst. Why has Dickens suddenly taken off this way? The answers are probably multiple, because Dickens was here, as always, trying to serve several purposes and answer all of his public and private needs at one time. He was entertaining by describing, but thought his description of the poor children of London might yield a moral-social-political message as well, so he uses this occasion to provide it. He is also expressing his own personal dissatisfaction at a world where children are allowed to slink like rats. But his rhetoric dare not be too strong or too specific, lest it upset or offend his audience. T. H. Lister is probably representative of that audience, and he praised Dickens because there was in his novels

> no mawkish wailing for ideal distresses – no morbid exaggeration of the evils incident to our lot – no disposition to excite unavailing discontent, or to turn our attention from remediable grievances to those which do not admit a remedy.[5]

Bagehot's judgement was that Dickens began by describing really removable evils 'in a style which would induce all persons, however insensible, to remove them if they could; he has ended by describing the natural evils and inevitable pains of the present state of being in such a manner as must tend to excite discontent and repining'.[6]

The fine line Dickens needed to walk here in his rhetoric should be obvious. Were children slinking like rats a 'remediable' evil? Or was Dickens to be accused of 'exciting discontent and repining'? Dickens's authentic personal concern for these children seems self-evident. But equally self-evident is the fact that he tries to dispel it – to chase the discomfort away – with words. But no matter how intense the rhetoric, it is finally impotent; its insistence itself evidence that it is at the mercy of the encroaching reality it was meant to chase away. Thus the reader is left feeling both aware of a social evil and urged most strongly to do something, and yet absolutely bereft of any suggestions of what he might do; is provided no comfort save impotent threat. Bagehot claimed that Dickens's reflections were 'perhaps the worst reading in the world', and insisted that 'no writer [was] less fitted for an excursion into the imperative mood'.[7] Dickens did have some very specific notions of what legislation was desirable – he certainly knew where he stood on international copyright laws, for instance – but the fact is that even if he had had more specific social and political recommendations to make, he may well have feared to make them and risk losing his audience. 'In the great English novels of the eighteenth and nineteenth centuries,' says Wolfgang Iser,

> one has the feeling that the author's remarks are made with a view not to interpreting the meaning of the events but to gaining a position outside them – to regarding them, as it were, from a distance. The commentaries, then, strike one as mere hypotheses, and they seem to imply other possibilities of evaluation than those that arise directly from the events described.[8]

In such cases, then, commentary does not diminish the interpretive work the reader must do, but instead increases it.

There are other times when the rhetorical energy of Dickens's novels seems not only unsuited to the imperative mood, but unfocused as well. Chapter II of *Little Dorrit*, for instance, opens with Arthur Clennam, just returned from twenty years in India, on his way 'home' to a dreary house he is not particularly eager to reach. Dickens takes this occasion to lead us on another walk through the streets of London at night, and to comment rhetorically on what it is we see as we pass those streets:

> It was a Sunday evening in London, gloomy, close, and stale. Maddening church bells of all degrees of dissonance, sharp and flat, cracked and clear, fast and slow, made the brick-and-mortar echoes hideous. Melancholy streets in a penitential garb of soot, steeped the souls of the people who were condemned to look at them out of windows, in dire despondency. In every thorough-fare, up almost every alley, and down almost every turning, some doleful bell was throbbing, jerking, tolling, as if the Plague were in the city and the deadcarts were going round. Everything was bolted and barred that could by possibility furnish relief to an overworked people. No pictures, no unfamiliar animals, no rare plants or flowers . . . all taboo . . . . Nothing to see but streets, streets, streets. Nothing to breathe but streets, streets, streets. Nothing to change the brooding mind, or raise it up. Nothing for the spent toiler to do, but to compare the monotony of his seventh day with the monotony of his six days, think what a weary life he

led, and make the best of it – or the worst, according to the probabilities.

> At such a happy time, so propitious to the interests of religion and morality, Mr Arthur Clennam, newly arrived from Marseilles by way of Dover, . . . sat in the window of a coffee-house . . . . Ten thousand responsible houses surrounded him frowning as heavily on the streets they composed, as if they were every one inhabited by the ten young men of the Calender's story, who blackened their faces and bemoaned their miseries every night. Fifty thousand lairs surrounded him where people lived so unwholesomely, that fair water put into their crowded rooms on Saturday night, would be corrupt on Sunday morning . . . . What secular want could they possibly have upon their seventh day? Clearly they could want nothing but a stringent policeman [LD.I.iii.28–31].

The description goes on, of course, for a good long time. It has all of the ingredients that we recognise in Dickens's prose: the animated and wilful objects, the allusions to fairy tale and legend, the balanced sentences, the catalogue, the mesmerising repetitions, the vivid reportage of actual locations. But if we look more closely at the passage we can see that besides the vivid evocation of mood and the careful specificity, what seems most worth noticing is the way description shades off into rhetoric; becomes almost indistinguishable from rhetoric. What we have here is not simple description or narration at all, but inextricably tied up with these things an attack on city administrators who have decreed that places of amusement be closed to the working classes on Sundays. (Dickens's 'Sunday under Three Heads' was an attack on just this practice.) What we have also is an attack on the 'ignorant county member' who is so indifferent to the filth and pollution of the environment in which the people live. What we have is an attack on organised religions that offer nothing but dreary church services to a people who need clean air, and if not that, at least something like real solace. And what we have, finally, is an attack directed at nobody at all: an outburst against Fate, or against Monotony, or Dreary Sundays, and rain. It is true, of course, that Dickens is describing this scene from the vantage point of Arthur Clennam, and he is restless and generally dissatisfied, and so the scene and the attitudes in it are in part Clennam's, and the restlessness and dissatisfaction partly his. But so far as we know, Arthur Clennam has no particular concern for the lack of amusement facilities for the poor in London. He has no particular interest at the moment in cleaning up the polluted waters, or in informing ignorant county members of the danger of allowing the poor to live in filth. That dissatisfaction is Dickens's own. What the reader must feel at such times is something like what Leavis recognised: insistent intention, but intention that is taken up in no inclusive way, and failing to inform the novel as a whole. The urgency the reader must feel in such instances is that of a subject – Dickens – needing to express his feelings, more than the urgency of objects individual enough to need or demand expression.[9]

Perhaps no one has come so close to tracing the cause, in Dickens, of this phenomenon than G. K. Chesterton, who says in his study that

> Dickens had all his life the faults of the little boy who is kept up too late at night. The boy in such a case exhibits a psychological paradox; he is a little too irritable because he was a little too happy. Like the over-wrought child in society, he was splendidly sociable, and yet suddenly quarrelsome. In all the practical relations of his life he was what the child is in the last hours of an evening party, genuinely delighted, genuinely delightful, genuinely affectionate and happy, and yet in some way fundamentally exasperated and dangerously close to tears.[10]

What Chesterton refers to is the account of how the young Charles Dickens was often called upon late at night to stand atop a table and sing comic songs for the entertainment of his father and his companions. What we have in the novels, Chesterton suggests, is that same over-tired child who is both exuberant and grumpy at the same time, or by swift turns first one and then the other. We have enough evidence from the letters Dickens wrote to know that Dickens, certainly from the time of the writing of *Dombey and Son* on, did often admit to feeling 'giddy' and 'restless'. He confides to Forster at one point that 'if I couldn't walk fast and far, I should just explode and perish.'[11] While he was writing part 3 of *Little Dorrit*, he says that in that part 'I have been blowing off a little indignant steam which would otherwise blow me up.'[12] It is this giddiness, irritability, restlessness, this need to expound or explode, which often takes the form of insistence upon some action (usually unspecified), that evidences itself time and time again in Dickens's rhetoric, and those critics who talk of Dickens's 'excess of energy' may well be responding in part to the uncontrolled, undirected rhetorical energy often found in those rhetorical flights.

There are, in fact, times when these rhetorical admonitions run absolutely counter to what he provides in his plots. In *Bleak House*, for example, there is an extensive rhetorical warning to the wealthy and the powerful. If they do not take the responsibility for cleaning Tom-all-Alone's upon themselves, Tom-all-Alone's will repay them by sending its filth and infestation up to their mansions. (The rhetorical tactic is not new. Carlyle, for instance, in *Past and Present*, calls it a wise economy to help the poor Irish widow dying of typhus, because 'if you don't she will prove her sisterhood; her typhus will kill [you]'.) So in *Bleak House* Dickens announces

> Tom-all-Alone's has his revenge. Even the winds are his messengers, and they serve him in these hours of darkness. There is not a drop of Tom's corrupted blood but propagates infection and contagion somewhere. It shall pollute, this very night, the choice stream (in which chemists on analysis would find the genuine nobility) of a Norman house, and his Grace shall not be able to say Nay to the infamous alliance [BH.xlvi.627–8].

This is a very persuasive rhetorical warning. But what happens in the plot is that it is Esther, who has ministered faithfully to the poor and the sick, who contracts Jo's smallpox and is left disfigured, and not the people of 'the Norman house' or 'his Grace' who have ignored him. It is easy to see here the truth of George Bernard Shaw's observation that Dickens's 'sentimental assumptions are violently contradicted by his observations'.[13] Dickens would like to believe and would have us believe that ours is a rational universe and a moral universe, where the good are rewarded and evil punished. But his honest observations of the universe around him would not support his belief. So again and again he *tells* us, in his rhetoric, one thing, and *shows* us, in his plots, quite another. This is probably the fate of all novelists who choose to be both descriptive and prescriptive. The same kinds of disharmonies can be found between rhetoric and vision and rhetoric and plot action in the novels of Theodore Dreiser, for instance. On the first page of *Sister Carrie* Dreiser announces that

> When a girl leaves her home at eighteen, she does one of two things. Either she falls into saving hands and becomes better, or

she rapidly assumes the cosmopolitan standard of virtue and becomes worse. Of an intermediate balance, under the circumstances, there is no possibility.[14]

But in fact during the course of the novel Carrie falls into neither of Dreiser's two categories. In what ways does she become 'better', and in which ways 'worse'? The truth is, she simply becomes what she becomes, and the moral rhetoric (if we assume better and worse are moral categories) is simply inappropriate and out of harmony with the reality described so well otherwise in the novel. For Dreiser as for Dickens, the moral rhetoric may have been intended to contain the reality being conveyed, but that moral rhetoric is never comprehensive enough or complex enough to handle the vision. And the result is that the very accurate renderings of experience tend in yet another way to spill over their rhetorical containers.

3 THE RETICENT RHETORICIAN

> If commentary is not supplied, there is in the text a kind of *degré zéro* of 'commentary' . . . [and] the receiver of the message is then under a strong compulsion to supply the commentary felt to be missing, that is, to replace the absent 'commentary' in the text by an act of 'interpretation' of his own.[1]

If there are times when Dickens's rhetoric or that of his narrators seems excessive, times when it seems inadequate or inappropriate to the action, and times when it runs counter to the action provided in his plots, there are also times when Dickens or his narrators provide no rhetorical help at all, leaving the reader to deduce for himself what responses might be appropriate to the scenes Dickens has created.

Chapter XXVII of *Little Dorrit* has bothered me for a long while. It has caught the attention of Robert Garis and the Leavises as well. In this chapter, Mr Meagles confronts Miss Wade and pleads with her to encourage Tattycoram to return to his home and to her function as companion and servant to his daughter 'Pet'. Tattycoram had run away from the Meagleses feeling that she had not been properly appreciated, but more than that, feeling that she, too, is as deserving of love and 'petting' as Pet is. The issue here is really whether Tattycoram – or any servant – is justified in defying a master and benefactor; if a young servant girl might be as deserving of love as Pet Meagles. The scene is a long one, and one would expect that Dickens's own sympathies would show through. But they don't. Instead, the rhetoric is filled with *seems, whethers, perhaps, ifs, appears, may have beens,* and *might have beens,* at the rate of at least four per page throughout the scene, or thirty-seven in all. Mr Meagles begins by admitting that Pet 'may have been a little more inconsiderate than usual in requiring services' [LD.I.xxviii.322] of Tattycoram. Of her running away, he says 'It seems as if it was to be' [LD.I.xxviii.322], but, he adds, 'it might have been borne by Tattycoram' [LD.I.xxviii.322].

Robert Garis looks at this *might-* and *seems*-infested scene and concludes that 'Dickens's grasp of the whole Meagles family and what they represent is always uncertain and distinctly inept.'[2] The Leavises look at this same scene, attack Garis for assuming that Mr Meagles's speech about duty to one's master is being 'endorsed' by Dickens, and explain that what we are supposed to see here is that Dickens was 'both admiring and censorious of' the Meagles family.[3] Their impulse to be practical people, to take in and care for an orphan, is admirable. But not their innocent snobbishness or their failure to consider that Tattycoram might have sensitivities and needs equal to those of Pet. Dickens's kind treatment of Mr Meagles is seen by the Leavises as 'giving a harmless sop to the Meagles section of the reading public that would give them the moral they could understand while allowing the novel's meaning to sink in perhaps . . . at another level'.[4]

The Leavises' judgement on Dickens's rendering of moral here is admirably kind. But it would seem to me that, for a writer who expressed again and again his intention to try to change people's minds and hearts, who thought he could help humanise people and alert them to the problems of prostitutes by 'turning [people's] thoughts a little that way' in *Oliver Twist,* and 'putting [the subject] before the thoughts of people in a new and pathetic way, and perhaps doing some good' in *David Copperfield,*[5] who was pleased to be able to expose the evils of the Yorkshire schoolmasters in *Nicholas Nickleby* and a whole host of other social and economic evils elsewhere, the moral here is pallid at best, and bears none of the force that Dickens's putative statements about his moral and social and political intentions might lead us to expect. As Gérard Genette tells us, commentary is unnecessary only if the narration itself proceeds by agreed-upon canons, and if it illustrates usual, predictable and understood behaviours.[6] Dickens's moral stance might be regarded as clear here, then, only if we all agreed that no words were necessary on the proper attitude to hold toward servants and their rights and needs. This is not the case, however, and as Ross Chambers suggests, 'where comment is absent, the interpreter's first task is to identify the reason for its absence.'[7] Because of Dickens's evasive or reticent rhetoric here, we can never really know exactly where Dickens's sympathies lie in this scene and all others like it. Ought servants to be treated with dignity and gentility, or were they to be given speeches about 'duty' by their masters? Was Dickens afraid to offend the Meagles segment of the population as the Leavises contend, or did he in actuality share their sentiments himself? In largest part, we cannot know, and at such points the reader in the Dickens world becomes, yet again, a reader at work.

There are other times when this is so, and specifically, these times often occur when one or another of Dickens's characters espouses a point of view about which neither Dickens nor his narrators express any opinion whatsoever. In the inn in which Rigaud stops to eat, he encounters the lady of that establishment expressing her notions of the nature of human nature and the way in which she believes 'evil' people are to be treated:

> I tell you this, my friend, that there are people (men and women both, unfortunately,) who have no good in them – none. That there are people whom it is necessary to detest without compromise. That there are people who must be dealt with as enemies of the human race. That there are people who have no human heart, and who must be crushed like savage beasts and cleared out of the way [LD.xi.127].

These are pretty strong words, and one would expect that Dickens, concerned as he was for changing feelings and attitudes towards criminals, would take some position in response to the innkeeper's sentiments. But he does not. The rhetorical intervenor who is so strongly outspoken about some things remains curiously silent. Instead, the narrator says only that

> the landlady's lively speech was received with greater favour at the Break of Day, than it might have elicited from certain amiable whitewashers of the class she so unreasonably objected to, nearer Great Britain [Ibid.].

Where does this statement leave us, and where are we to assume Dickens is in all this? One might expect to find clues in the narrator's attitude toward this character on other occasions. But in fact she disappears from the novel and is never heard from again. The truth of the matter is probably that a part of Dickens really did feel as the landlady of the Break of Day did. And that another part of him did not. So Dickens, like Mark Tapley, 'comes out strong' by fracturing his own opinions, putting one point of view in the mouth of one character and another in the mouth of another, commenting rhetorically on none of them, and thus having it all ways at once.

The phenomenon of the morally unavailable narrator generates other effects as well:

> 'Halloa, sir!' growled the schoolmaster, turning round. 'What's that, sir?'
>
> 'Nothing, please sir,' said the little boy.
>
> 'Nothing, sir!' exclaimed Mr. Squeers.
>
> 'Please sir, I sneezed,' rejoined the little boy, trembling till the little trunk shook under him.
>
> 'Oh! sneezed, did you?' retorted Mr. Squeers. 'Then what did you say 'nothing' for, sir?'
>
> In default of a better answer to this question, the little boy screwed a couple of knuckles into each of his eyes and began to cry, wherefore Mr Squeers knocked him off the trunk with a blow on one side of his face, and knocked him on again with a blow on the other [NN.iv.31–2].

There is no rhetorical intervention here, and none is needed. Here is Dickens at his best, recreating man's inhumanity to man – or child – and some men's temptation to sadism (a common target, in the Marquis in *A Tale of Two Cities* and in Gamfield in *Oliver Twist*). In fact, *Oliver Twist* is particularly full of horrific recreations of injustice and cruelty, without any cry of outrage from the narrator at all. Bumble explains why two sick pauper children are to be taken away by coach:

> They are both in a very low state, and we find it would come two pound cheaper to move 'em than to bury 'em – that is, if we can throw 'em upon another parish, which I think we shall be able to do, if they don't die upon the road to spite us. Ha! Ha! Ha! [OT.xvii.120].

Psychologically, what happens to the reader at such points as these must be powerful. We are provided no relief in the person of a moral voice in the novel that cries out at the crimes described. Instead, the reader must provide the outrage, since the narrator is quite matter-of-fact as he relates his tales of horror. When we might think we need him most, the narrator is curiously absent, allowing us to carry the whole weight of moral outrage on our shoulders. This happens time and again: in descriptions of the Gordon Riots in *Barnaby Rudge*; in Phil Squod's descriptions of how he came to be so scarred as a child in *Bleak House*:

> I was passable enough when I went with the tinker, though nothing to boast of then: but what with blowing the fire with my mouth when I was young, and spileing my complexion, and singeing my hair off, and swallering the smoke, and what with being nat'rally unfort'nate in the way of running against hot metal, and marking myself by sich means; and what with having turn-ups with the tinker as I got older, almost whenever he was too far gone in drink – which was almost always – my beauty was queer, wery queer, even at that time. As to since; what with a dozen years in a dark forge, where the men was given to larking; and what with being scorched in a accident at a gas-works, and what with being blowed out of winder, case-filling at the fire-work business; I am ugly enough to be made a show on [BH.xxvi.367].

In all of these instances moral outrage – or outrage against Fate – surely overtakes the reader after he has read the narrator's dispassionate accounts. Since that outrage seems also to catch up with us only after the fact, it is compounded by our own outrage at ourselves, for not noticing in the instant what it is we are hearing and seeing – and even laughing at. Without a narrator as a kind of moral cheerleader, we find ourselves passing by the poor and the abused and neither noticing nor caring particularly – until we stop ourselves short and realise exactly what it is we have been passing by.[8]

Oftentimes, Dickens's narrators abandon us to our own outrage partly as a result of the fact that they have become characters in the novels themselves. They are at times not only not the agency by which social or moral commentary is admitted into the novels, or not a means of providing ironic distance, but instead they become

simply one more character for us to contend with. The narrator of
Dombey and Son, particularly in the earliest chapters of that book, is
quite as deferent to the power of Dombey as are many of the other
characters in that novel. When he reports Dombey's actions, he is as
awed and humble before the great Dombey as is the nurse present at
Paul's birth, who, when Dombey asks her her name, responds
submissively, 'Blockitt, Sir?' as if it were up to Dombey to decide
whether to accept her name, or give her another. The narrator's
accounts of Dombey are full of qualifiers; hesitancies: 'These and
other appearances of a similar nature, had served to propagate the
opinion that . . .' [DS.i.7]; 'To record of Mr Dombey that he was
not in his way affected by this intelligence [of his wife's death] would
be to do him an injustice. He was not a man of whom it could
properly be said that he was ever startled or shocked. . . .' [DS.i.5].
The narrator describing the mysterious Mr Tulkinghorn is as
reserved, as cautious, as is Tulkinghorn himself. He suggests rather
than tells. He covers his tracks, makes tentative statements that he
can retract should he need to. He reports of Tulkinghorn that he is

> habitually not uncensorious and contemptuous perhaps. The
> peerage may have warmer worshippers and faithfuller believers
> than Mr Tulkinghorn, after all, if everything were known
> [BH.xxvii.376–7].

The rhetoric of the narrator of *Oliver Twist*, in the earlier pages of
that book particularly, is quite as dissociated from the sufferings of
the characters as anyone could be, referring regularly to the
newborn Oliver as an 'item of mortality', or as 'it' rather than 'he'.[9]
At times this narrator adopts the tones and attitudes of what one
presumes are the most indifferent members of the upper classes, as
the narrator reports

> Although I am not disposed to maintain that the being born in a
> workhouse, is in itself the most fortunate and enviable circum-
> stance that can possibly befall a human being, I do mean to say
> that in this particular instance, it was the best thing for Oliver
> Twist that could by possibility have occurred. The fact is, that
> there was considerable difficulty in inducing Oliver to take upon
> himself the office of respiration, – a troublesome practice, but
> one which custom has rendered necessary to our easy exist-
> ence [OT.i.1].

In fact the narrator at times becomes so much a character in the action that his reports and descriptions become as vague, confused and partial as would be the reports of one who is in the middle of those events he describes.[10] Oftentimes, the narrator can provide no more than an account of what he has heard from others, since he himself does not know what is happening. During the scenes describing the Gordon Riots in *Barnaby Rudge*, for instance, most of our information comes to us second-hand; as miscellaneous gossip the narrator has gathered from here and there:

> Some of the insurgents said that when it ceased, they heard the shrieks of women, and saw some garments fluttering in the air, as a party of men bore away no unresisting burdens. No one could say that this was true or false, in such an uproar [BR.lv.423].

Not only does the narrator report no more than what he heard from others, but the grammatical form of that report is in part litotes, that by its very nature seems both to affirm and deny at the same time. In such cases, when the narrator's reports are full of what 'someone said', but what no one can affirm positively or deny absolutely, the reader always confronts a world made up, as Paul Goodman suggested, of a 'continuum of the ordinary, the plausible, the odd, the wonderful, and the preturnatural'.[11] Confronting the 'someone said', the reader needs to be constantly alert to the fact that what is reported may be true or false, commonplace or fantastical, believable or improbable. Prefacing reports with 'some said' makes the reader also inclined to feel that events are 'actual . . . and yet inexplicable'.[12] As most recent literary theory would have it, such reports also constitute a kind of 'foregrounding' of language, so that the reader's attention is drawn to language itself, rather than to whatever is being conveyed in that language. We are drawn to observe not only the tale itself, but the process of tale-telling as well. Nowhere do we feel more poignantly the inability to know everything, or to know what to do for our fellow human beings, than we do when the narrator says of poor Miss Flite, who carries her reticule to court day after day, year after year, hoping for a settlement from the Court of Chancery, that we know will never come: 'Some say she really is, or was, a party to a suit; but no one knows for certain, because no one cares' [BH.i.3].

It is in the narrator's refusal to let us know the whole truth, and in his admission that he doesn't *know* the whole truth, that the power of this kind of passage lies. In Dickens's novels there is always side by side both an insistent rhetoric – insistence that we do something to improve the condition of the common man – and a reticent rhetoric – which suggests that no one, not even the narrator, has a clear idea of what is happening. Under the circumstances, doing anything becomes a bit difficult: even figuring out how how to respond to the Dickens world becomes a bit difficult.

It is probably in part this reticent rhetorician in Dickens's novels that prompted George Henry Lewes, and other critics, to regret that Dickens was 'all surfaces', by which I presume he meant that Dickens often refuses to let us in on the psychological workings of his characters' minds, or to posit reasons for their behaviour. But at times Dickens makes his narrators deliberately reticent. In *Oliver Twist* there is an extensive passage about how human beings are 'meant to be a mystery to each other', and about 'the secret workings of the human heart'. So, although it is true that sometimes, as in Dombey's case, the narrator in a Dickens novel exposes the interiors of hearts in a sentence, at other times the narrator tells us, as he does of Mrs Clennam in *Little Dorrit*:

> What scenes and actors the stern woman most reviewed, as she sat from season to season in her one dark room, none knew but herself [LD.I.xxix.339];

and of Amy Dorrit:

> What her pitiful look saw, at that early time, in her father, in her sister, in her brother, in the jail; how much or how little of the wretched truth it pleased God to make visible to her, lies hidden with many mysteries [LD.I.vii.71];

and of Lady Dedlock in *Bleak House*:

> It may be that my lady fears this Mr Tulkinghorn, and that he knows it. It may be that he pursues her doggedly and steadily, with no touch of compunction, remorse, or pity. It may be that her beauty, and all the state and brilliancy surrounding her, only gives him the greater zest for what he is set upon, and makes him the more inflexible in it. Whether he be cold and cruel, whether immovable in what he has made his duty, whether in love of power, whether determined to have nothing hidden from him in

ground where he has burrowed among secrets all his life, whether
he in his heart despises the splendour of which he is a distant
beam, whether he is always treasuring up sleights and offences in
the affability of his gorgeous clients, whether he be any or all of
this, it may be that my lady had better have five thousand pairs of
fashionable eyes upon her . . . than the two eyes of the rusty
lawyer [BH.xxix.402];

and of Manette;

Whether he knew what had happened, whether he recollected
what they had said to him, whether he knew that he was free,
were questions which no sagacity could have solved
[TTC.II.vi.46].

As Paul Goodman suggests, it may be that the alternatives posed by
all of these *whethers* suggest a continuum along which truth lies, to be
found – somehow – by the reader. It may be that the narrator would
like to suggest that the truth is complex, and that all of those
alternatives have something of truth in them to recommend them.
But it may be true that the narrators are confessing in their rhetoric
sheer and honest bewilderment and inability to know anything with
any certainty. In spite of the narrator's zeal for description, and his
readiness to credit surfaces with significance, there are simply some
things that we cannot know. This, I think, is yet another source of
the real mystery in Dickens's novels. Dickens reserves, finally, what
he calls 'the mystery of the human heart'. Often enough, the
narrator's rhetoric lapses into sequences of *seemses*, *perhapses*,
confessing that the best he can do is provide some notion of what
appears to be true.

4 THE RHETORIC OF 'SEEMS'

We saw, or fancied we saw, it makes no difference which.[1]

But seeming may be false or true.[2]

It was either the fact too, or he fancied further.[3]

Dickens's rhetoric is sewn together with *seems*. Such constructions as *seems, might have been, may be,* or such phrases as 'appeared to be' or 'he fancied' are, of course, to be expected in great profusion on the pages of a mystery story. Insofar as the writer increases the frequency of such words and phrases, he increases the possibilities for misleading his readers and preserving his mystery and increases the possibilities for generating dramatic irony. But the rhetoric of *seems* in Dickens's novels goes beyond this.

When Arthur Clennam 'fancies' that the Dorrits don't treat Amy Dorrit very well, that fancy is to be understood to be perfectly true, and an accurate perception of her situation. When the narrator of *A Tale of Two Cities* remarks that it 'appeared rather agreeable to [the Monseigneur] to see the common people dispersed before his horses, and often barely escaping from being run down' [TTC.II.vii.103], we know that this 'appeared' signals what is also true, though what perhaps for delicacy's sake, since what is being expressed is the man's latent sadism, Dickens couches in 'appears'. When Mr Boffin plays miser, Bella Wilfer is said to see 'a cunning light in his eyes as he said all this, which seemed to cast a disagreeable illumination on the change in him, and make it morally uglier' [OMF.III.v.475], and that 'seems' serves to perpetuate the 'mystery' of the novel. When the narrator tells the reader of *Bleak House* early in the novel that on everything at Chesney Wold 'there seemed to be such undisturbed repose' [BH.xviii.246], we learn later that here, too, we have been misled, for at Chesney Wold Lady Dedlock hardly experiences much real 'repose'. In fact, much later in that novel, Esther reminds us of how we have been misled, as she refers us to

> the old house . . . on which there had seemed to be such complete repose, when I first saw it, but which now looked like the obdurate and unpitying watcher of my mother's misery [BH.xxxvi.513].

These last are the *seemses* dictated by Dickens's mysteries, and their revelation as false clues brings about the resolution of the mystery. But once one has sifted out from the rhetoric of the novels the *seemses* and *appears* that denote that which is true, and those that provide false clues, there remains a pretty large residue still to be accounted for.

When Pecksniff is exposed as the hypocrite he is, for instance, the narrator announces that at that precise moment 'not only did his figure appear to have shrunk, but his discomfiture seemed to have extended itself even to his dress. His clothes seemed to have grown shabbier' [MC.lii.810]. This strikes me as an instance of yet another order of seeming or appearance, in which *seems* signals that which is emotionally or metaphorically true, even if not, finally, visually or physically true; what is true to the spirit rather than true to some external reality. Further, this description, like Esther's of Chesney Wold, shows us how much what we 'see' is altered by our apprehension of what cannot be 'seen'. Chesney Wold once 'seemed' to exhibit repose. What it 'seems' to exude now is obduracy and unpitying vigilance. Chesney Wold looks no different, but in Esther's perception of it, it *has* changed. Pecksniff hasn't really changed either. But he does *seem* to have changed. Rosa Dartle's thinness 'seem[s] to be the effect of some wasting fire within her' [DS.xx.292], says David Copperfield, and that *seems*, too, denotes something that is more real than not. When Dickens says of Fagin that

> he glided stealthily along, creeping beneath the shelter of the walls and doorways, the hideous old man seemed like some loathsome reptile, engendered in the slime and darkness through which he moved: crawling forth, by night, in search of some rich offal for a meal [OT.xix.135],

again what seems to be is what feels true to the spirit. When Eugene Wrayburn and Mortimer Lightwood follow Rogue Riderhood, they notice that the footprints he leaves behind are 'mere shapeless holes; one might have fancied, following, that the very fashion of humanity had departed from his feet' [OMF.I.xii.157].

In these last examples, however, what we have is even more than some kind of emotional reality described, but moral judgement masquerading as reportorial objectivity. The narrator cannot say for sure, but what 'seems to be' is . . . . And what follows the 'seems to be' is to be taken as truth. Wayne Booth describes Faulkner doing the same thing in his novels:

> Modern authors have often managed to give an acceptable air of objectivity while reaping all the benefits of commentary, simply by dealing largely with the appearances, the surfaces, while allowing themselves to comment freely, and sometimes in seemingly wild conjecture, on the meaning of those surfaces. 'Upon the book Hightower's hands are folded, peaceful, be-

nignant, almost pontifical,' says the narrator of Faulkner's *Light in August*. This novel shows Faulkner as a master of the conjectural description which is really not conjectural at all.[4]

Dickens is also a master of this same kind of directed description. Rosa Dartle's thinness may 'seem' to be the result of some wasting fire within her. It not only seems to be; it is. Her own misdirected passion is in fact, as well as in seeming, consuming her substance. Pecksniff really *has* shrunk in stature. Rogue Riderhood really *is* becoming more beast and less human. So in Dickens's novels what is proferred as the unknowable, the mysterious and unascertainable, is in fact often anything but those things.

As often as not, the *seems* in Dickens's rhetoric is followed immediately by an analogy in the form of *as if*, and very soon the sharp reader comes to see that when Dickens's narrators say that something 'seems as if', they are again being directed to feel one way or another about whatever is being described. Sometimes the *as if* serves, as Professor Sucksmith observes, as a kind of foreshadowing or prophecy,[5] but as Wayne Booth suggests, the device of having the narrator couch his description in the form of *as if* may also 'serve general realistic demands – it is "as if" the author really shared the human condition to the extent of not knowing for sure how to evaluate events. But morally the effect is still a rigorous control over the reader's own range of judgement.'[6] Under the guise of the *as if*, then, Dickens again imposes judgement. When the Marquis rides through the village at top speed in his carriage, sending children scrambling out of his path, he is described as coming 'as if he came attended by the Furies' [TTC.II.viii.108]. We are to understand that Miss Wade's influence on Tattycoram is pernicious 'when the narrator describes her as putting 'her arm around [Tattycoram's] waist as if she took possession of her for evermore' [LD.I.xxvii.330], an analogy full of echoes and overtones of demonic possession.

To accept Dickens's rhetoric or that of his narrators is to surrender oneself to the proposition that the seen and the felt reality are one and the same. Dickens gives the game away when, in 'Meditations in Monmouth Street' he reports that 'we saw, or fancied we saw, it makes no difference which' [SB.II.vi.76]. In some degree, for Dickens it *didn't* always matter which. To see or to fancy was all one and the same. This is certainly true in cases such as that of Dickens's defending Krook's spontaneous combustion: such things *really did happen*, Dickens protested, himself failing to make the distinction between imaginative and actual realities. To look at surfaces and to draw conclusions and make evaluations on the basis of what those surfaces 'seem' or 'appear' to mean is also one, continuous activity. Perception and moral judgement take place simultaneously.

But once the reader surrenders himself to Dickens's logic – that the *seems to be* and the *is* are synonymous, that surfaces reflect moral truth – he is in what is potentially a very complex realm. For what happens when, for whatever reason, we cannot or will not agree with the narrator's analysis or interpretation of those surfaces? The reader is quite prepared to accept the emotional validity of some of Dickens's *seemses*. He is also quite prepared to enjoy Dickens's mystery stories, and play the game of separating the true *seemses* and appearances from the false ones in order to solve the mystery. But the reader must also decide which of those *seemses* that denote the presence of moral judgement on the basis of interpreted surfaces he is willing to accept as truth, and which he is not. And that is a whole different realm of mystery. To look at Dickens's portrayal of Slackbridge, for instance, is to become aware of how description and evaluation have become inextricably mixed, and to become aware, further, of how much at the mercy of the narrator and his morality the reader is. To Dickens, Slackbridge seems an 'ill-made, high-shouldered man, with lowering brows, and his features crushed into an habitually sour expression'. He wears 'mongrel dress'. He never laughs but with 'disdain', or 'sarcasm', or 'bitterness' [HT.II.iv.138–44]. But the reader may not be so sure that he would have perceived Slackbridge in that way at all, and is not so sure he is ready to accept this portrait as an accurate one of a union man. He may also not be prepared to think of Miss Wade's influence on Tattycoram as in any way a kind of demonic possession – even if Miss Wade is a Lesbian. Ross Chambers suggests that there are four kinds of interpretive acts necessary at any time at which 'commentary' of an explicit nature is absent from a text: recuperative (providing a context when commentary is absent); redundant (the kind of commentary we provide in a teaching situation when we ask 'what does the writer mean by X?'); restorative (the kind of commentary we provide when we re-introduce empirical data that has become outdated and no longer readily available to the interpreter); and defamiliarising (in which we try to 'defamiliarise' commentary which goes unnoticed because it seems so close or 'natural' in the attitudes it conveys).[7] In the case of these last instances, in which Dickens provides very strong commentary slipped in under a *seems*, the reader is involved in what must be yet a fifth kind of interpretive act. What would have had to be 'defamiliarised' by the Victorian interpreter has to be somehow the object of exactly the reverse activity by the modern reader. Dickens's analogies are arbitrary, of course, as all writers' are. But in Dickens's moral world, in which separating the 'good' people from the 'bad' people seems so important, the reader must always remain exceedingly alert, deciding which of Dickens's analogies that carry with them moral judgement he is willing to accept as accurate renderings, and which he feels compelled to reject. Dickens's reader is, then, once again a reader at work, and the energy of the novels is again, partly that of the reader.

5 The World beyond the Dickens World

About suffering they were never wrong,
The Old Masters; how well they understood
Its human position; how it takes place
While someone else is eating or opening a window
or just walking dully along.[1]

'But,' says Mrs Harris, the tears a-fillin in her eyes, 'you knows
much better er than me, with your experienge, how little puts us
out. A Punch's show, a chimbley sweep, a newfundlandog, or a
drunkin man a-comin round the corner sharp, may do it.'[2]

Most of the action in *David Copperfield* takes place in carefully
circumscribed locales: around the hearthside at Blunderstone, at
the Peggottys' cosy houseboat, at Betsey Trotwood's cottage, or at
the Wickfields' home. But for brief spaces of time, while David
makes his way to Betsey Trotwood's after running away from his job
at Murdstone and Grinby's, the reader encounters quite another
and a different world. David tries to pawn his jacket to get money to
buy some bread, and in doing so he finds himself having to contend
with a strange old man 'with . . . trembling hands, which were like
the claw of a great bird', who shrieks at him, grabs him by the hair,
and repeats, 'Oh, my eyes and limbs, what do you want? Oh, goroo,
goroo!' [DC.xiii.184]. David extricates himself from this strange
man after much time and difficulty, runs down the highway, only to
encounter a young tinker who interrupts his beating of his wife just
long enough to steal David's scarf from around his neck, and then
resume knocking her about again [DC.xiii.187–8]. David is as
sanguine about such episodes as any child might be expected to be,
for he is used to meeting with mystery in the streets, whenever he

leaves the hearthside of those who care about him. Earlier, as he was being taken to Salem House, he had stopped off to eat with Mr Mell, and had met the strange Mrs Fibbitson, who appeared at Mr Mell's fireside just long enough to shake a fist at David for stealing some of the warmth of her fire before receding back into the shadows, never to be heard of again [DC.v.75]. The young street urchin David had hired to carry his box for him had gone rattling off with both the box and all of David's money, never to be heard of again, once his hysterical laughter stopped echoing in David's ears – and ours. Quite as much as Little Nell or Oliver Twist, David Copperfield expects to meet strange creatures in the streets.

I have chosen *David Copperfield* to illustrate as dramatically as possible that even there, in that warmest and in some ways least mysterious of Dickens's novels, there exists another and more mysterious world at the peripheries of the novel: a world where strange creatures are likely to lurch at us without warning, as if out of the shadows. Like the great tin grotesques in the funhouses we stumbled through as children, there are in all of Dickens's novels characters that seem to pop up at us from out of nowhere, shout, shake their fists at us, grab at our clothes, and then recede back into the darkness. Amy Dorrit is accosted in the night by a strange woman who seems to be a procuress after stray children. Edith Dombey finds herself grabbed by an old lady who would tell her fortune. Florence Dombey almost loses her hair to a strange old woman who kidnaps her and wants to steal her hair and her shoes.

For the most part, the phenomenon of the peripheral character has gone unremarked. Those critics whose interest is in elucidating patterns in Dickens's novels naturally ignore them, because they do not readily pattern. For the rest of us, some general comment as to how Dickens's imagination was of a kind that could never resist adding just one more character has seemed to be a sufficient explanation. We content ourselves with trading favourites from among them: the 'youngish, sallowish gentleman in spectacles, with a lumpy forehead' in *Our Mutual Friend*, who says in a raised voice at the Podsnaps' party, 'ESKER' [OMF.I.xi.132], seems to be a particular favourite. The aunt who appears at the wedding reception for the Lammles' 'glaring petrifaction' at Lady Tippins [OMF.I.x.121] is another. My own favourite is Mrs Sprodgkin, who drives poor Reverend Milvey to distraction by taking his ministerial 'call-on-me-anytime' as literally as it is possible to take it [OMF.IV.xi.746–8]. (Actually, it is the Imp of the Perverse in me that makes me prefer her. In fact, she's not in the novel at all, except by report, much like Sairey Gamp's Mrs Harris.)

For so long as we continue to regard all of these extra characters individually, however, or simply as comic interludes, we shall miss an important source of some of Dickens's strongest effect on readers. To begin to say how these characters do generate meaning in readers, however, we need to look first at how they get into the novels, since the road by which they reach us often determines what their effect on us will be. We might begin by comparing Dickens's busy novels with those of Gogol, a writer also known for his ability to conjure up large numbers of characters. In *Dead Souls*, when Chichikov enters the Governor's residence to attend a formal ball, the black frock-coats of the men in the hall flash by

> like flies on a gleaming white sugar loaf on a sultry July day as an elderly housekeeper breaks it into shimmering splinters in front of an open window: the curious children gather to watch the movements of her roughened hands as they lift the mallet while the soaring squadrons of flies, riding in on the light air, land boldly as if they owned the place, and taking advantage of the old woman's poor sight and her being blinded still further by the sun, scatter over the tasty pieces, here singly, there in heaps. Sated during the opulent summer, they come flying, not to eat really, but to show themselves, to swagger up and down over the sugary heap, to rub their front and back legs together. . . .[3]

Later, when Manilov nods, he is said to nod

> like a music lover when the operatic soprano outdoes the violin itself and lets out a note so high-pitched it even exceeds the capacity of a bird's throat.[4]

Gogol likens a group of soldiers, coachmen and workers to 'ladies in red shawls, their stockingless feet in town shoes, who flit around corners like bats'.[5] The brilliance of the images and the liveliness of the prose can easily obscure the simple but significant fact that neither the flies, the elderly women, the music lover, the operatic soprano, or the ladies in red shawls are on Gogol's stage at all: they are pure figures of speech.

Among Dickens's characters, Sam Weller in *Pickwick Papers* is always calling up other people in his analogies, much as Gogol does:

I only assisted natur' ma'am; as the doctor said to the boy's
mother, arter he'd bled him to death [PP.xlvii.664].

There; now we look compact and comfortable, as the father said
ven he cut his little boy's head off, to cure him o'squintin
[PP.xxviii.384].

It's over and can't be helped, and that's one consolation, as they
always says in Turkey, ven they cuts the wrong man's head off
[PP.xxiii.315].

But Sam Weller and Sairey Gamp are pretty much the only
characters in Dickens's novels whose creatures are conjured up
purely in language. All the other peripheral characters who find
their way into Dickens's novels, the old pawnbroker who cries
'goroo, goroo', Mrs Fibbotson shaking her fist by the fireside, the
wandering procuress, these are not simply figures of speech. They
are *there*, they wander into the novel on their own steam, are just as
'real' as Oliver, as Little Dorrit, or Little Nell, real enough to reach
out and grab the coat-sleeves of the unwary wanderer through the
streets of Dickens's world. They cannot so easily be dismissed with
the kind of laugh with which we can dismiss Sam Weller's
capricious physician.[6]

Our expectations are that after the first few chapters of a novel,
the population of that novel will remain stable. New characters
added after that point are assumed to have some particularly
startling reason for being there: they arrive to clear up mysteries, or
to solve crimes. But in the world of a Dickens novel one must
contend not only with thirty or fifty characters, as if this weren't
enough, but with a constantly increasing population. It is easy
enough to say that although Dickens became a master of creating
complicated plots, elaborate structures for accounting for all of his
miscellaneous detail in the end, he still had at the same time the
opposite impulse to write picaresque tales like those he had read as a
child, and that thus he wrote carefully plotted novels with the
intrusion of picaresque characters. But the literary or formal
explanation hardly accounts for the effect such a practice has on the
reader of this peculiar mixture of the structured and the planned,
and the miscellaneous. It should be obvious, for instance, that the
Dickens world approaches more nearly the feeling of the real world,
since, in the world of his novels as in life, we are never sure where

and when a new human being will enter our line of vision, and equally unsure whether these new people will demand attention and reaction, or whether we can afford to ignore them. Dickens's novels in this way are a simulacrum of life, which never has a stable cast of characters, and in the novels although a good many people turn out to have rather elaborately contrived ties with a good many other people, some characters simply pop up out of nowhere, and go back to the same place. Some of these characters we meet and then lose in the space of a page are benevolent, as the turnpikeman and the old lady who feed Oliver Twist [OT.viii.52]. Some are as evil as the wife-beater in *David Copperfield*. Some seem frightening. Little Dorrit and Maggy encounter in the streets 'homeless people lying coiled up in nooks. They had started from slinking men, whistling and signing to one another at bye corners, or running away at full speed' [LD.I.xiv.174]. But who knows whether such creatures are 'dangerous', or whether they are not. Some who, like Miss Pross, rush on stage 'wild-looking' and having on her head 'a most wonderful bonnet like a grenadier wooden measure, and a good measure too, of a great stilton cheese' [TTC.I.iv.25] turn out to be quite harmless, in spite of their strange initial appearance. Some of these abruptly entering characters return later to play some larger part in the novel in which they appear. The strange fortune-teller who accosts Edith Granger early in *Dombey and Son* turns out, of course, to be Mrs Brown whose daughter Alice Marwood is a shabbier version of Edith herself [DS.xxvii.381]. The bull-like boy who butts Pip at Miss Havisham's house on his first visit there turns out to be one of Pip's best friends, Herbert Pocket. But others of the characters that move in and out of our line of vision simply disappear, having no apparent ties with anyone. They are no one's long-lost brother, and they carry the key to no mystery of parenthood. They are simply there. And part of the mystery generated by Dickens's novels is to be traced to the reader's efforts at separating those peripheral characters that will return from those that will not; those that hold the key to some mystery, from those that do not.

GE

That so many of these peripheral characters are of the lowest social classes is significant as well, and conducive to a genuine sense of mystery in the novels that exceeds that generated by the plot. Kenneth Burke, for instance, suggests that mystery arises at any point at which different *kinds* of beings are in communication. 'The conditions for mystery are set,' he suggests,

by any pronounced social distinctions, as between nobility and
commoners, courtiers and king, leader and people, rich and poor,
judge and prisoner at the bar, . . . Thus even the story of
relations between the petty clerk and the office manager,
however realistically told, draws upon the well of mystery for its
appeal, since the social distinction between clerk and manager
makes them subtly mysterious to each other.[7]

So even if or when there is no plot mystery, Dickens's novels
frequently strike the reader as full of mystery insofar as these ragged,
peripheral characters reach out and grab the coat-sleeves of a
person of another class: Florence Dombey or David Copperfield, for
instance. Obviously, Rose Maylie and Nancy's encounter at the
steps of the bridge at night is inherently 'mysterious', and if
Dickens's novels strike us in memory as complex and mysterious,
this is in part true because the kind of mystery generated in and by
such peripheral characters is not of a kind that will ever be – or can
ever be – solved.

   There is a second class of peripheral characters who enter the
world of Dickens's novels only by the report of other characters, and
do not actually appear on Dickens's stage at all. Here, too, it is their
mode of entry into the novel that is responsible for generating
powerful effects on the reader. In *Oliver Twist*, for instance, a whole
world of mystery and misery and evil far beyond that which we
encounter at the centre of the plot enters our consciousness through
the report of other characters, and as often as not by the report of
unsympathetic characters indifferent to the miseries of those whose
stories they recount.[8] Thus Bumble, the beadle, recalls that he first
wore his parish coat with the Good Samaritan buttons 'to attend the
inquest on that reduced tradesman, who died in a doorway at
midnight' [OT.iv.21]. From Bumble we also learn about the
husband whose wife died after he refused some medicine 'given in a
blacking-bottle off-hand' because it 'wouldn't suit his wife's com-
plaint'. Bumble says that it was 'good strong medicine, given with
success to two Irish labourers and a coalheaver' [OT.v.30].
Flintwinch reports that his brother 'speculated unsuccessfully in
lunatics, he got into difficulty about over-roasting a patient to bring
him to reason, and he got into debt' [LD.II.xxx.783]. There are,
then, always in Dickens's novels great misfortunes, miseries and
injustices happening somewhere at the periphery of his stage, and
we often learn of them only by report, and often distorted in the

telling by an unsympathetic reporter. Mrs Sapsea is dead long before the opening pages of *The Mystery of Edwin Drood*, and we learn about her only from her oafish husband's report [MED.iv.36]. What really happened to her? Did Sapsea really effectively kill her with his heavy hand and heavy moralisms, as we suspect? What really happened to that reduced tradesman Bumble tells us about so off-handedly? And was the medicine given to the man for his wife really the right medicine after all? We shall wonder, but we can never really know. Who is Dorker, who died at Dotheboys Hall, and what really happened to him, anyway? [NN.iv.36].

So much of misery enters the peripheries of the Dickens world by the side-door of report. We learn of the six dead Crisparkle babies only accidentally and by the way when Septimus Crisparkle mentions that he is called Septimus 'because six little brother Crisparkles before him went out, one by one, as they were born, like six weak little rush-lights, as they were lighted' [MED.vi.49]. Gaffer Hexam relates without passion the story of the bodies he has dredged up from the deep:

> two young sisters what tied themselves together with a handker-cher. This is the drunken old chap, in a pair of list slippers and a nightcap, wot had offered – it afterwards come out – to make a hole in the water for a quartern of rum stood aforehand, and kept to his word for the first and last time in his life [OMF.I.iii.22].

Sarah Gamp and Mr Gamfield report their own cruelties perpetrated off-stage, and although our initial response to their stories is bound to be laughter, were we to see Sarah Gamp in action, comforting the sick ('Bite a person's thumbs, or turn their fingers the wrong way . . . and they come to, wonderful [MC.xlvi. 709]), we would most certainly feel more repelled than amused. Or, as James Kincaid suggests, we would both laugh at such escapades and accounts, and then feel immediately guilty for laughing.[9]

Getting our information only by the report of other characters, distanced from the events they record both in time and in space, the reader is bound to feel as helpless and as powerless, as unable to really know the truth, as we feel when we read the morning papers. Injustices are reported, and we know both that they have been distorted in the telling so that we have no way of knowing what actually happened, and that we are powerless to correct those injustices. This feeling of not being in possession of nearly all the facts, of having no possibility of ever comprehending the whole, that is a part of the source of our feeling that the Dickens world is a world of richness that exceeds that generated by the plot. Furthermore, by maintaining as much distance from the scene of these crimes and accidents of Fate as he does, Dickens avoids having to castigate the criminals, and he avoids even rhetorically blaming the guilty, as he is compelled to do with actions that happen at the centre of his stage rather than on the peripheries.

What the constant references to other people do, most simply, is serve as a constant reminder that the world on which our attention is focused by the plot and the narrator is not the only world or the whole world. There are other worlds constantly impinging, and we are left recognising that they, too, are real. While David Copperfield pays a visit to Omer the funeral director, Joram is at work, 'this minute, on a grey [coffin] with silver nails, not this measurement' [DC.xxi.304]. He is constructing a child's coffin. Those critics whose interest lies in illuminating structure and pattern will be quick to recognise in this episode a foreshadowing of the death of David's baby half-brother, because, of course, at that time another coffin of small dimensions will be built. But one can call this scene a foreshadowing without ignoring the fact that the scene does other things as well. In fact, our most elemental response must surely be something like a recognition that at the same time David pays a friendly call, there are people somewhere grieving for the lost baby who will soon be laid to rest in that coffin.

When the Dorrits, newly rich, enjoy the luxury of warmth and food in a mountain hostel in Switzerland during their travelling about Europe, the narrator tells us how

> while all this noise and hurry was rife among the living travellers, there, too, silently assembled in a grated house, half-a-dozen paces removed, with the same cloud enfolding them and the same snowflakes drifting in upon them, were the dead travellers found upon the mountain [LD.II.i.433].

This vignette attracts the attention of the Leavises, who say that 'it is impossible (for the reader, I mean), to have forgotten the potent evocation of time, eternity, the non-human universe, the derealising lights and vapours, and death. The effect is to bring out with poetic force the nothingness of the Dorrit-Gowan-Barnacle human world.'[10] Sylvia Manning says of this same scene that 'the frozen travellers present the outward form of the spiritual state of the living travellers.'[11] Both of these are plausible readings of the scene. But it is also plausible to say that what is more simply true is that here Dickens has created two very *human* (rather than 'non-human' as the Leavises say) worlds, and that the scene of frozen travellers serves to make us aware that as large as the panorama of life Dickens provides us is, it is still but a small fraction of the whole. While we play, others grieve, and while we are grieving, others play. The poor man who pleads for food and is given a lump of coal in *Oliver Twist*, and who wanders off to die in the night, trails after him our sympathy and our recognition that a crueller world does exist, as well as our recognition that there is little we can do to help him. Arthur Clennam has miseries enough of his own, but when we meet him in the night, 'passing silent warehouses, and wharves, and here and there a narrow alley leading to the river, where a wretched little bill, FOUND DROWNED, was weeping on the wet wall' [LD.I.iii.31], not only Arthur Clennam, but we, too, are reminded of miseries far beyond those we can see. Just as we follow and try to solve Dickens's mystery stories and absorb his images almost subliminally, we also, while following Dickens's characters and his plots, absorb his peripheral world in the same way. We may not even be completely be aware of either the images or the peripheral characters that flit by so rapidly. Nonetheless, the allusions to coffins for dead babies, to drowned bills 'weeping on the wet wall', to murdered lunatics, must arouse some kind of generalised discomfort as they accumulate, perhaps all the more so as we do not fully recognise the source of that discomfort as we read.

Why do we find so many off-hand and off-scene references to miseries in Dickens's novels? Few writers are as little help as Dickens in explaining what he did or thought he was doing. His letters to Forster are full of references to his latest novel, and he does talk about what he is doing, but often the best and most we can learn is that he thinks of his newest novel as 'droll', or as 'a pretty idea'. We can speculate, however, on what that peripheral world might be doing by sifting out other commentary from other sources. Obviously, when Dickens wanted to point up moral or social evils, he felt it necessary to be very careful lest he offend his audience. From all that we can gather, he was wise to do so. Lady Carlisle, for instance, is reported to have said upon reading *Oliver Twist* that she 'knew there were such things as pick-pockets and street-walkers', but that she 'did not much wish to hear what they say to one another'.[12] Lord Melbourne's account of his reactions to that same novel suggest that he, too, was more than a little reluctant to face moral or social uglinesses. 'It is all among workhouses and pickpockets and coffinmakers,' he says. 'I do not like them in reality and therefore do not like to see them represented.'[13] It seems safe to assume that if some Victorian readers didn't care for pickpockets or streetwalkers, they could hardly be expected to hold still for starving paupers and dead babies, and that is why Dickens slipped them in via the peripheral world.

Dickens hardly considered his mission to be only that of the bearer of ill-tidings, however. He also wanted to 'sweeten the lives and fancies of others', as he told Angela Burdett-Coutts.[14] He wanted not just to tell his Victorian audience who was suffering and why, but he also wanted to entertain them. And he wanted to entertain them, in part, with portraits of all of those 'humans warious' he saw on the streets of London. As Steven Marcus says so aptly, Dickens was bitten by that great bug of the Victorians, 'heroic pedestrianism'.[15] When he felt restless, he took solace in walking the streets at night. For part of the time in which he was composing *Dombey and Son*, he was on vacation in Lausanne, Switzerland, and he confessed to John Forster that he had trouble writing there because of 'the absence of any accessible streets'[16] in which to wander. The streets and the sights he saw there entertained him, and diverted him from his restlessness. What he found in the streets of London at night was diversion, but diversion in the shape of a great many suffering human beings wandering those same streets. This is how it is that one of the most profound effects of Dickens's novels is generated. We, like Dickens, are being entertained and diverted, but with portraits of very real suffering humanity. They are people Dickens really saw on his rambles through the streets at night, and because they were in his head, they make their way into the pages of his novels. They are not part of the plots, they play no role in the mystery, and they have most often no direct – or even indirect – relation to the main characters. Still, in their accumulation, their effect on the reader is profound, and must, in truth, be exactly the same effect they had on Dickens the man. Forster shrewdly observed of Dickens that

> there was for him no 'city of the mind' against outward ills, for inner consolation and shelter. It was in and from the actual he still stretched forward to find the freedom and satisfactions of an

ideal, and by his very attempts to escape the world he was driven
back into the thick of it. But what he would have sought there, it
supplies to none; and to get the infinite out of anything so finite,
has broken many a stout heart.[17]

Dickens leads us out into the streets to divert and to entertain us,
bringing momentarily into our line of vision an unending parade of
miscellaneous human beings. And although they do provide
diversion, at precisely the same time they remind us of exactly those
things we most needed escape and diversion from. And as Forster
says so well, in our attempts to escape that world, like Dickens, we
find ourselves being driven back into the thick of it.

2 THE HUDDLE

I, hungry, thirsty, weary. You, imbeciles, where the lights are
yonder, eating and drinking and warming yourselves at fires.[1]

The night was bitter cold . . . . Bleak, dark, and piercing cold, it
was a night for the well-housed and fed to draw round the bright
fire, and thank God they were at home; and for the homeless
starving wretch to lay him down and die. Many hunger-worn
outcasts close their eyes in our bare streets, at such times, who, let
their crimes have been what they may, can hardly open them in a
more bitter world.[2]

The 'thick' of Dickens's London is an awesome, confusing and
fearsome place. Wandering the streets at night, characters are
almost bound to encounter at least one mysterious, grotesque figure
whose intentions seem in some way vaguely or explicitly threatening. Esther Summerson describes her trip through 'the dirtiest and
darkest streets that ever were seen in the world', and 'in such a
distracting state of confusion that [she] wonders how the people kept
their senses' [BH.iii.28]. Barnaby Rudge's father, a 'houseless,
rejected creature', wanders about the streets 'imagining the happy
forgetfulness each house shuts in' [BR.xviii.138], and when he takes
refuge in his wife's hovel and is warned that he must leave because
Barnaby is coming home, he answers that he fears Barnaby less
'than the dark, houseless night' [BR.xvii.130]. When the wandering
David Copperfield must sleep in the streets, he chooses to sleep

outside the windows of Salem House, so that at least he can feel
somewhat near to the warmth and companionship he had previously known [DC.xiii.183]. Little Nell and her grandfather hope
in some vague way that by running to the country they will find
escape from the dangers that have surrounded them as city
wanderers. Harriet Carker's home rests at the edge of the city, and
she can often be found in *Dombey and Son* sitting by the window
watching stragglers who come wandering into the city

> footsore and weary, gazing fearfully at the huge town before
> them, as if foreboding that their misery there would be but as a
> drop of water in the sea, or as a grain of sea-sand on the
> shore . . . . Swallowed up in one phase or another of its immen-
> sity, towards which they seemed impelled by a desperate
> fascination, they never returned. Food for the hospitals, the
> churchyards, the prisons, the river, fever, madness, vice, and
> death, – they passed on to the monster, roaring in the distance,
> and were lost [DS.xxxiii.480].

The city is a monster, 'roaring in the distance', where the innocent,
the naïve and the unsuspecting are as likely as not to be 'swallowed
up'.

How is one to survive in this fearsome place? One can certainly
take some comfort in the pastoral pleasures of the country. In fact,
Dickens's 'bad' characters are nearly always to be distinguished
from his 'good' characters by the fact that the good people can
appreciate and enjoy nature, and the bad do not. (*Martin Chuzzlewit*
is full of scenes in which we are introduced to Tom Pinch
appreciating nature, and Jonas Chuzzlewit ignoring it.) Nothing is
quite as delightful to Dickens or his narrators than coming upon a
bit of nature or a bit of country in the midst of the city. In *Edwin
Drood* there is

> one of those nooks, the turning into which out of the clashing
> street, imparts to the relieved pedestrian the sensation of having
> put cotton in his ears, and velvet soles on his boots. It is one of
> those nooks where a few smoky sparrows twitter in smoky trees, as
> though they called to one another, 'Let us play at country'
> [MED.xi.112].

The key word here, however, is *play*. One can play at country, one can take comfort in and return to the country periodically for a kind of purification and rebirth, but one needs, finally, to work out one's destiny in the city. From that there is no escape. Wemmick has his fairy-tale like retreat from the city and the business world, complete with garden and moat, but it is only a temporary retreat, and when morning comes he has to return to the city to earn his bread. When Miss Tox is sad, she tries to take pleasure in remembrance of the pastoral pleasures of her youth:

> She fell into a softened remembrance of meadows, in old time, gleaming with buttercups, like so many inverted firmaments of golden stars; and how she had made chains of dandelion-stalks for youthful vowers of eternal constancy, dressed chiefly in nankeen; and how soon those fetters had withered and broken [DS.xxix.409].

But her relief is, like Wemmick's, only temporary. In the midst of the reverie the present and the city impinge, and the flowers of her pastoral reverie are transformed into those of the flower-hawker in the street:

> [He] came crying flowers down Princess's Place, making his timid little roots of daisies shudder in the vibration of every yell he gave, as though he had been an ogre, hawking little children [DS.xxix.409].

This is an example of what Leo Marx calls 'the Sleepy Hollow motif'. At the same time that Thoreau was creating his pastoral retreat in the woods at Walden Pond, he could hear the screech of locomotives just beyond, and because of that intrusion he knew, just as Dickens knew, that the pastoral retreat was no longer possible.[3] Nature is nice, but it provides no antidote to the evils of the city. How then is one to survive in the city, since there is no escaping it?

The answer is one so completely dissolved in Dickens's plots that it becomes his one great theme. One can endure life in the real, bewildering world of the city by huddling together around the hearth and protecting one another from what is fearsome – and beastlike – in the world outside. Alexander Welsh talks in *The City in Dickens* about the significance of the hearth in the context of sexuality and 'the rediscovery of the religion of the hearth in the nineteenth century' in general,[4] but the hearth and the huddle around the hearth has political implications as well. What all the food and feasting is about in all of Dickens's novels is not hard to figure. Eating and drinking are very serious ceremonies that bind those who partake together, and protect them from the great unknown outside. Nothing consoles the Micawbers, ravaged by fate and failure, like a hot bowl of punch shared with friends.

Among other things, protecting one another means regarding with warmth, understanding and humanity one another's madnesses. Mr Dick is treated as a trusted friend and adviser by Betsey Trotwood, in spite of the fact that in her heart she knows he is quite mad. Flora Finching's gentle attention to Mr F's Aunt is little different from Amy Dorrit's toward her father, or Estella's for Miss Havisham, and both of those young people know, too, that their charges have a tenuous grip on a real world. Mrs Chick at least tolerates her husband's periodic outbursts of 'rump-te-iddity bow-wow-wow', even if they don't make her particularly happy – especially as they come during a funeral. Mrs Gummidge's tearful recitation of her troubles as a 'lone lorn creetur' are accepted by the Peggotty household with bemused affection. All human beings, whether drunk, or mad, or sick, are to be sheltered and protected from the world by their family and fellows. The good woman or the good wife is 'quiet and good' like Agnes Wickfield, who protects her man – father or husband – from the world outside. The good child is one, like Jenny Wren, who will – even though with a sharp tongue – protect a drunken father.

The hearth and home are sacred institutions whose function is protective and exclusive. To violate that institution is a great crime. Dickens's own attachment to hearth and home could hardly have been stronger. How else can we easily explain the peculiar domestic arrangements made after his separation from Mrs Dickens, an arrangement whereby he kept all but his eldest child with him, immediately setting up a household with Mrs Dickens's sister Georgey as mistress in charge of the house and children. The great sin of Dombey and the Murdstones is not only pride, or a vicious righteousness, but the rejection and driving out of daughter and son from their rightful home. Little Em'ly sins as much in the running-off as she does in running off with a man. She has abandoned the accepting fires of the Peggotty home, something even crazy Mrs Gummidge knows better than to do, for when Mr Peggotty proposes going off to Australia with Em'ly, she cries, 'Doen't ye think of leaving me behind, Don't! Oh, doen't ye ever do it'

[DC.li.739]. Silas Wegg's villainy lies in not accepting, without treachery, Boffin's opening of his hearth and home – not to mention his pantry – to him.

If sin is driving out inheritors from their hearth, hell is finding oneself driven out and wandering, as Little Nell, or Nancy, or Betty Higden, or Oliver Twist all do. In nearly every novel, Dickens is careful to give us glimpses of those 'people out of doors'. That phrase itself had become a kind of catch-phrase at the time of the Poor Law Amendment and the Chartist agitation of the 1830's. Each time he gives us a portrait of those people out of doors, he is careful to rhetorically insist that we in our own comfortable homes should open up, and become aware of the suffering on the streets. Again and again Dickens intervenes in his novels to say

> Oh for a good spirit who would take the house-tops off . . . and show a Christian people what dark shapes issue from amidst their homes, to swell the retinue of the Destroying Angel as he moves forth among them! . . . Not the less bright and blest would that day be for rousing some who never have looked out upon the world of human life around them, to a knowledge of their own relation to it, and for making them acquainted with a perversion of nature in their own contracted sympathies and estimates [DS.xlvii.648].

As Betty Higden wanders about the streets, Dickens cries out

> Those gentlefolks and their children inside those fine houses, could they think, as they looked out at her, what it was to be really hungry, really cold? [OMF.III.viii.505]

Every novel has some such outburst, and each is interchangeable with any other, and the substance of each is the same. Dickens is urging an 'opening-up' to the world of suffering outside our doors. But at war with that sentiment is Dickens's own urge to retreat; to huddle around the hearth, eating, drinking with family and friends, shutting out both the fearsome city and the responsibility for our fellows that awareness of their suffering brings. What Dickens's characters *do*, and what Dickens rhetorically advises that we do, are really two very different things. Even the best among Dickens's characters are largely oblivious to the suffering humanity they pass by in the streets. Mr Brownlow takes in one orphan, and so do the

Boffins. Gabriel Varden involves himself with the Rudges, and Arthur Clennam is seen giving a few spare coins to a cache of young girls huddled in a doorway in the rain. But all of the rest, charming and human though they be, are constantly shutting their doors on suffering humanity. The impulse to shut out is understandable, of course. To open up our doors to the world means to become aware of a great deal of misery. The good Mr. Pickwick asks to take a walking tour of the Fleet Prison to get to know his new neighbours. When he does, his sympathetic soul is stunned by the squalor, turmoil and noise until at last he cries out desperately, 'I have seen enough . . . . My head aches with these scenes and my heart too. Henceforth I will be a prisoner in my own room' [PP.xlv.645].

Nearly all of Dickens's novels, seen in and from this perspective, end the same way: with his heroes and heroines prisoners in their own rooms, huddled around the hearth, literally quite as often as figuratively. Dombey is last seen stroking the head of his grand-daughter before the fire. Esther Summerson and her doctor have their own fireside. So do the newly married Clennams. Most of the people in *Our Mutual Friend* end in the same way. Sol Gills and Cap'n Cuttle smoke their pipes before the fireside once again at the end of *Dombey and Son* and we feel, if the truth be told, that that is just as it ought to be.

Still, at the same time Dickens makes sure we cannot ignore cries like that of Rigaud, who is shut out from any hearthside. As he approaches the lighted and inviting windows of the Break of Day tavern he grumbles

I, hungry, thirsty, weary. You, imbeciles, where the lights are yonder, eating and drinking and warming yourselves at fires. I wish I had the sacking of your town; I would repay you, my children [LD.xi.124].

Hugh of Maypole in *Barnaby Rudge* insists that he is what he is – a drinker and a rioter – because he has been deprived of the circle of home fire. When Mr Chester accuses him of always being drunk he responds:

I always am. Why not? Ha ha ha! What's so good to me as this? What ever has been? What else has kept away the cold on bitter nights, and driven hunger off in starving times? What else has given me strength and courage of a man, when man would have left me to die, a puny child? [BR.xxiii.178]

There is a superfluity of evil and misery in the world, and Dickens is at great pains, rhetorically, to tell us that it is there partly because of our tendency to shut human beings out of the warmth of our hearts and hearths. Thus, finally we bear at least a part of the responsibility for what evils lurk in the city. If Hugh of Maypole is bitter and violent, it is partly our fault. If we would make the world a better place, we have to begin by opening our hearts to those whom we – or Fate – have shut out.

But if salvation for the world may lie in opening one's heart and hearth to others, simple personal survival may require just the opposite response. For who could bear to be receptive to all that suffering humanity outside? Thus in still another way Dickens's novels – in the contradiction between plot action and resolution, and rhetoric – embody what is a very rich and ambiguous response to life and living. It is a response that comes very near our own responses to our own moral dilemmas. We, too, feel both the urge to huddle and the urge to open up; the urge to be both expansive, and exclusive.

3 THE DOUBLE VISION

There is a pleasure from learning the simple truth, and there is a pleasure from learning that the truth is not simple. Both are legitimate sources of literary affect, but they cannot both be realised to the full simultaneously.[1]

The lines above are from Wayne Booth, but I am not so sure he is right. Dickens's novels, it seems to me, provide the reader with both pleasures, and in equal proportions. The vision of man both opening in heart and consciousness to the world outside himself, and huddled with a chosen few *against* incursions from without is not the only dual vision generated by and in Dickens's novels. Barbara Hardy's study of Dickens often points to many of the dualities of vision at work in his novels. Dickens's novels are a 'combination of social despair and personal faith', showing 'a capacity to distrust both society and social reform while retaining and perhaps deepening a faith in the power of human love'.[2] Dickens urges an opening-up and helping of one's fellows, and all the time holds up for our admiration the picture of those who help themselves. David Copperfield says quietly, for instance, 'I laboured hard at my book, without allowing it to interfere with the punctual discharge of my newspaper duties; and it came out and was very successful' [DC.xlviii.]. One hears Dickens himself very much in this quiet statement.

But there are other 'dual visions' at work in Dickens's novels. A great many Dickens critics have argued persuasively that as Dickens's novels unravel, they take in more and more social classes, account for more and more of what appear at first glance to be miscellaneous events and details. H. M. Daleski, for instance, talks about the way that the movement of the novels is like that of ripples created by a pebble thrown into a stream. The ripples move outward, taking in more and more space, encompassing more and more people and events in the ever-widening concentric rings.[3] The strange lady who accosts Edith Dombey is really Mrs Brown whose daughter has sold herself or tried to sell herself in marriage much as Edith is about to do. When we meet John Cavalletto and Rigaud in their Marseilles prison room, we have no doubt at all that we shall meet them again later in the novel, and we do. Critics who remark such careful interconnections between character and character, event and event, are fond of quoting John Forster, who says that curious chances always

> led Dickens to the saying he so frequently repeated about the smallness of the world; but the close relation often found thus existing between things and persons far apart, suggests not so much the smallness of the world as the possible importance of the least things done in it, and is better explained by the grander teaching of Carlyle, that causes and effects, connecting every man and things with every other, extend through all space and time.[4]

Monks and Oliver of course must turn out to be half-brothers; Lady Dedlock turns out to be Esther Summerson's mother; the old man who drowns himself for a quartern of rum in *Our Mutual Friend* turns out to be the father of Jenny Wren's father, the drunken Mr Dolls. In this last instance, the interconnection is so complex, and mentioned so off-handedly, I doubt that few readers ever catch it.

Those people who marvel at Dickens's ability to juggle so many characters and make them 'come out' and connect in the end often point to the page of notes extant in Dickens's hand for each part number of each of the novels, except for *Pickwick*, *Oliver Twist*, *Nicholas Nickleby*, *The Old Curiosity Shop*, *Barnaby Rudge*, and part of *Martin Chuzzlewit*, to show how carefully Dickens plotted his course each step of his way. Obviously, I admire with the rest of Dickens's readers his herculean accomplishments in tying together so many strands and bringing together so many characters. But we need to look again at John Butt and Kathleen Tillotson's description of the page of notes Dickens kept for each serial part of many of his novels, particularly in the middle of his career. Butt and Tillotson are very careful to say that on the basis of ink differences; i.e. differences between the left and right side of each of those pages, it seems clear that the left side was composed as a kind of exploratory listing of what he *might* write about in a particular number; the listing on the right side of the page was composed after he had written the number, to remind him of what he had done, and to prepare him to compose the subsequent number.[5] What this means is that Dickens left himself plenty of elbow room in which to add in lots that was not necessarily part of his master plan. He not only followed some precise plan, but also and quite as much wrote what came into his head in the heat of creative fury, and a great many characters and events in the novel are there not because they fit some grand design, but simply because they came to his head and hand as he wrote. One can easily imagine the Dickens that his daughter Mamey describes, talking to himself, imagining new characters and new voices, alone in his room.

So, even if Dickens did want, as he said, to show the 'interconnectedness of all things', he also had the opposite but equally compelling impulse to describe what was in his head and what he saw around him: the nameless people who wander about the streets, and lots of other things as well. These people have no particular ties with any one of the major characters in the novel. Rather, they are in the novels because they exist in the real world and Dickens couldn't or didn't want to ignore them. He wanted them in his books whether they were 'consistent' with his moral theme and vision or not.

What this means is that there are in Dickens's novels two contradictory messages to be found: it is a small world, and events in one quarter have unexpected results and effects on quite distant people and places; but it is equally true that the world is – or at least seems – basically incoherent and miscellaneous. Part of the power of Dickens's novels comes from the force of both of these truths.

The simultaneous connectedness and incoherence of the universe is by no means the only dual vision that Dickens's peripheral characters and world engenders. Dickens wanted, as he said time after time, to increase the stock of harmless cheerfulness in the world. His moral, as George Orwell said, is one that 'at first glance looks like an enormous platitude: if men would behave decently the world would be decent'.[6] If the world would only behave as a Mr Brownlow or a Gabriel Varden, if individuals would only behave toward each other with simple Christian charity, the world would be in much better condition, in this moral world where the good are rewarded and the evil punished, and where individual acts of kindness make a difference. As a prescriptive writer, this was always Dickens's stance. But at the same time he had the opposite but equally compelling impulse to be simply descriptive, and if at the centre of Dickens's plots the prescriptive Dickens has *his* say, at the peripheries of the novel the descriptive Dickens has his. E. M. Forster criticised those novelists like Dickens who round off their plots with a 'flurry of weddings', what he calls the 'silliest' of all possible endings.[7] But even if Dickens does marry off a great many of his characters at the end of his novels, as a kind of reward for good behaviour, it is equally true that many of his characters do not figure in the great and general marrying-off that Forster contends effectively kills off characters for ever. What happens to Rosa Dartle, and to all of those other characters in Dickens's novels who presumably live out their lives in dreary and echoing houses? One feels certain that Sarah Gamp should be – and is – somewhere still treating her 'intractable' patients to a very close turn around the fireside to bring them round. And Miss Tox, disappointed in love and fortune, continues to endure, teaching hordes of Toodles children in lieu of those children she will never have.

There are, then, in another way still two quite different responses a reader of Dickens's novel must have at the end of reading any of the novels. The main characters do nearly always end happily. But intermingled with those happier endings are memories of others not nearly so bright. If Lizzie Hexam and Eugene Wrayburn end happily wed, and Bella Wilfer and John Harmon end up in the remodelled Boffin's Bower, we don't forget, if we have any memory at all, that Jenny Wren's father ends drunk, and then dead, on a

London street. If Florence Dombey and her father end happily, we do not forget that somewhere Edith lives out her life alone and in shabby surroundings, and that her counterpart Alice Marwood has died in poverty long before her time. Our joy at such events as Amy Dorrit's marriage, has to be tempered by our knowledge that a host of other characters in that and every other novel end not nearly so happily. Some die. Others simply endure. Surely the lingering feeling that *Oliver Twist* leaves with us is not primarily relief or satisfaction or joy that Oliver has been formally adopted by Mr Brownlow or that Rose Maylie is happily married, or that the 'mystery' of Monks' and Fagin's persecution of Oliver has been solved. What lingers is the knowledge that Fagin has been hanged, that Monks has died in prison in the New World, that Nancy has been murdered and Sikes hanged, that Oliver's pauper friend Dick has died, and that the den of thieves – exclusive of Charley Bates – go on thieving in the same old way, so far as we know. If on the peripheries of Dickens's novels the good are not always rewarded (Betty Higden dies in spite of her sturdy pride and self-reliance), the evil are not always punished. The Murdstones, when we last see them, are doing well enough, and continue to thrive in spite of the disasters they have helped create. For all we know the Podsnaps are fine too. If Bounderby is exposed, Stephen Blackpool dies, in spite of his virtue. For all we know, Gamfield has himself a new underfed pauper boy to 'hextricate' from 'chimbleys' by setting his feet afire.

What we expect of a fictive world that contains 'evil' is that evil, or potentially discomfiting or threatening information, will somehow be contained and controlled by the artistic form. When fiction evokes a world that poses a threat to our security or peace of mind by reminding us of the evils that lurk in our own world, or suggests that our own actions may not have the results we desire, or that evil may flourish and good people suffer, then, as Simon Lesser says, that fiction may also

seek to enclose the terror in a kind of frame, to remind us that however powerful and triumphant evil may momentarily appear to be, its dominion is limited. Just beyond or outside this world of evil, fiction manages to inform us, there is a world of goodness, sanity, and health, where the normal rhythms of life prevail and one does not have to remain forever on guard against danger and disaster.[8]

The significant fact here is that Dickens in fact *reverses* this expectation. In his novels it is the 'world of goodness, sanity, and health' that occupies the centre of the novels. The plot always revolves around the 'good' people. That world at the centre of the novels is patterned, controlled by the plot mystery and its resolution, and given further form and pattern by images and symbols, and by expectations raised and then fulfilled. But the peripheral world, a world far more fearful and threatening in its implications, is *not* brought under artistic control, and does not partake of the pattern at the centre of the novels. Neither does it create its own pattern. I may not be the first reader of Dickens to prefer – emotionally if not rationally – the security of Mr Dorrit's prison room to the fearful – because vague and unknown – world of the streets that Amy Dorrit wanders outside the prison. What is vague, dimly perceived and not clearly defined is certainly disconcerting. 'The more a work grows in definiteness in the thought and under the hand of the artist, the more it will repress and subdue the chaotic tumult of emotional excitement.'[9] Dickens's peripheral world, by its very nature and by Dickens's own accounts, came to him 'ready made to the point of the pen', and because this is so, it is never brought under the complete conscious control of the artist. Thus if the novels feel full of excessive energy and mystery as critics have been saying for a century, that energy and mystery is to be traced in part to our own attraction to and fear of the peripheral world, a world where easy moral categories do not hold sway, a world where things just happen, without apparent rhyme or reason, and, as often as not, without justice.

It is safe to say, I think, that few but the most attentive readers could relate the details of the mystery surrounding Oliver Twist's birth and parentage. Or the specific details by which the Dorrit family comes into its wealth. Or for what reasons John Harmon comes to disguise himself for so long. Or the details of finance by which Carker brings about the downfall of Dombey. Nonetheless few writers strike us as so full of mystery, and this is so because intentionally or unintentionally Dickens has hit upon the psychologically most effective form he could possibly have chosen. In choosing to write mystery stories as he does, Dickens engages our intellect in solving his plot mysteries and trying to anticipate all of the interconnections between people and events. At the same time, however, he frees our unconscious to enjoy a whole stream of images and a whole peripheral world which might otherwise be so discom-

fiting that we might reject if we could. Norman Holland describes
the dynamics of this situation very well:

> The riddling form engages our processes of intellection; in
> technical terms, the ego's secondary-process or problem-solving
> thinking. The riddling form busies us with solving the riddle and
> incidentally enables less relevant, less presentable thoughts
> prompted by the joke [or the mystery] to sneak up on us, to take us
> unawares, as it were. So with the puzzling film. Its enigmatic
> promise of 'meaning' not only draws and holds our attention to
> the film; it also distracts us from the real source of our pleasure in
> the film, the thoughts and desires it evokes.[10]

Holland sees the mystery or the 'riddling form' as a way of diverting
our conscious attention so that our unconscious can be free to accept
the 'real meaning' of the fiction – which is the psychoanalytic. But it
seems to me there are other discomfiting facts that need to be
brought into our line of vision only peripherally, or may only be
'smuggled in' under cover of a plot mystery that will divert our
conscious attention. The plot mystery provides the onwardness, the
forward motion that keeps us reading. While we are engaged
solving riddles of plot or image or coherence, trying to find out what
things 'mean', we meet – almost without noticing it – Dickens's
parade of suffering, feeling, enduring humanity. And by some
mysterious sleight of hand, the mystery consequent upon Dickens's
mystery plots seems to be transferred to the mystery of life and living
in the city. Who and why are all of these people skirting my world,
and what, if any, is my connection with them, and furthermore,
what is to be done to and for them? As Geoffrey Hartman suggests,
'a central if puzzling feature of popular mystery is that its plot idea
tends to be stronger than anything the author can make of it.[11] Plot
is always only what E. M. Forster called the 'logical intellectual
aspect' of the novel. Plot requires mystery, and the mystery requires
to be solved or resolved in the end. Still, at the same time, the reader
is 'moving about in worlds unrealised',[12] and it is in the worlds
unrealised – rich, vague, mysterious – that much of Dickens's power
lies. Kenneth Burke has suggested that our success at solving plot
mysteries in a novel may serve 'homeopathetically' as a kind of
satisfaction and pleasure. Solving the plot mystery, we feel somehow
that we have solved puzzles imposed on us by conditions beyond our
control; have solved mysteries or puzzles that we cannot in reality

solve at all.[13] We may not have, as we read Dickens, solved the 'puzzles' of poverty and disease and crime and of lumbering institutions such as the Court of Chancery, but as we solve the plot mysteries of Dickens's novels, we may *feel* that we have.

4 THE TIME TELESCOPE AND THE LABYRINTH OF THE CONDITIONAL: THE EXPANDING WORLD IN TIME AND POSSIBILITY

We shall have his portrait if we picture to ourselves a man who, with a stewpan in one hand and a postillion's whip in the other, took to making prophecies.[1]

This sense of life's contradictions is a common sense and we take commonsensically that which if examined closely would turn into wonder and mystery, into a world of speculation, dense with *ifs* and *perhaps* and *might have beens*. We walk in the real world as Esther walks, through a labyrinth of the conditional.[2]

The Dickens world feels very large. It seems to extend itself in space, because of Dickens's peripheral vision. It extends itself in time, when Dickens's descriptions conflate past, present and future in what I shall call the 'time telescope', and it extends itself in possibility, largely, as we shall see, as a result of Dickens's constant use of the word *if*.

During Dickens's latter years at Gad's Hill, he chose to hang on the walls of his bedroom prints of Hogarth's drawings. What he admired in Hogarth was his ability to portray not only a social problem, but the causes which had led to that problem, and the results in the future should that problem not be alleviated.[3] Dickens tried to do with words what Hogarth did with pen and ink, bringing before the reader's attention not only misfortunes, but suggestions as to how those misfortunes occurred, and what might be expected to happen if one does not intervene to correct them. In *Little Dorrit*, for instance, he describes

wildernesses of corner houses, with barbarous old porticoes and appurtenances; horrors that came into existence under some wrong-headed person in some wrong-headed time, still demanding the blind admiration of all ensuing generations and determined to do so until they tumbled down [LD.I.xxvii.324].

Obviously, to describe only present conditions implies that things simply are what they are. Describing things through a kind of telescope that conflates past, present, and future, is to interject the notion that conditions, places, and people are all subject to change, and to interject the further notion that people can change conditions, places and other people. Dickens's descriptions make it clear that Tom-all-Alone's, Stagg's Garden, the desolate neighbourhood surrounding Todger's, the river slums around the Three Jolly Fellowship Porters, all are subject to change.

Telescopic description of characters serves another function. In the midst of some of Dickens's funniest descriptions of characters there is often very clear suggestion that in fact the physical deformity we laugh at was progressive, just as is the deterioration of the London neighbourhoods, and that it was caused by some fault of the character himself. Bounderby, for instance, has 'not much hair. One might have fancied he had talked it off; and that what was left, all standing up in disorder, was in that condition from being constantly blown about by his windy boastfulness' [HT.I.iv.14]. Flintwinch's 'natural acerbity and energy, always contending with a second nature of habitual repression, [gives] his features a swollen and suffused look; and altogether, he [has] a weird appearance of having gone about ever since, halter and all, exactly as some timely hand had cut him down' [LD.I.iii.37]. Partly Dickens is saying that people make themselves ugly. Krook has made himself look like a vampire by living off the substance and substances of others. Mrs Merdle resembles her parrot because she *is* a parrot, mouthing the principles of 'society'.

It is not possible for Dickens's readers to enjoy his scenes as artistic, static tableaux frozen in time, because even at the moment when people and places are being described, they are changing. Even Dickens's comedy is transformational: Lady Tippins's chin is 'on the way to a double chin; it might be called a chin and a half at present' [OMF.I.ii.10]. Silas Wegg has a wooden leg, but he is 'on his way' to a completely wooden body. If Dickens's imagic world suggests a world of shape-shifting beasts, a world transforming before our eyes, and if Dickens's shifting modes of presentation also suggest a world in which one must expect all to be transformed in the space of a paragraph, Dickens's descriptions, too, portray a world in the process of transformation.

Dickens's prose is also full of *ifs*. It may well be that any writer who sees himself as a describer and an advocate of change or transformation, as a prophetic proposer of a new social order, will make ample use of that word, since it provide a way to posit possibilities without becoming polemical. When Carker's sister hears Alice Marwood relate the details of her dreary life in and out of prison, for instance, she cries out, 'Heaven help you and forgive you,' to which Alice responds, 'If a man would help some of us a little more, God would forgive us all the sooner perhaps' [DS.xxxiii.482]. To Rose Maylie, who has been the only person to treat her with respect and dignity, Nancy cries out 'Oh, lady, lady! . . . if there was more like you, there would be fewer like me, – there would, there would! [OT.xl.301] Of M'Choakumchild in *Hard Times* the narrator muses, 'If he had only learnt a little less, how infinitely better he might have taught much more!' [HT.I.ii.8] There are hundreds of socio-economic-moral *ifs* in the novels. They suggest that specific changes – in human hearts, in attitudes, or in legislation – will bring about specific results. No matter how distressing the peripheral world of evil and misery, Dickens's refrain is always that things would be better *if*. At the same time that *Dombey and Son* gives us a picture of two people impossibly rigid in their convictions, and at the same time that their behaviour seems so inevitable and predetermined given the personalities and prejudices and upbringing of both, there is always the same refrain present in the novel: things could be better *if*. When Edith weeps for the first and last time in front of Florence, Dickens's narrator says, 'Had she been oftener thus in older days, she had been happier now' [DS.lxi.868]. The whole of Chapter 47 of *Dombey and Son* is made up of *ifs*, some implied, some explicit, but all of them suggesting that if a human being's nature is constricted, that person will respond by becoming as Dombey, one of 'contracted sympathies and estimates' [DS.xlvii.648].

Yeats, allegedly quoting from an 'Old Play', mused that 'in dreams begin responsibility'. In Dickens's world, it is also true that in possibility begins responsibility. Once one is aware that conditions can be altered, and that altered conditions will mean improved conditions for human beings, then one is morally responsible for bringing about those changed conditions. Thomas Carlyle's prose is as full of the conditional as are Dickens's novels, but his *ifs* as often as not signal either a nostalgic – and therefore free-of-responsibility – turning back to the past, or a flight into the purely conditional. They are statements much like those that begin 'If I were you', statements that carry with them no responsibility for action:

> If popular suffrage is not the way of ascertaining what the Laws of the universe are, and who it is that will best guide us in the way of these, – then woe is to us if we do not take another method.[4]

Thomas Jefferson used the same kind of conditional:

> If science produces no better fruits than tyranny, murder, rapine, and destitution of national morality, I would rather wish our country to be ignorant, honest, and estimable as our neighboring savages are.[5]

But where has it been proven that popular suffrage is *not* the way of ascertaining 'the laws of the universe'? And where has it been proven that 'science produces no better fruits than tyranny'? As a contrast to these hypothetical *ifs*, Leo Marx refers to the prose of Tench Coxe, a man who proposed, as Dickens often did, real, and not hypothetical *ifs* and alternatives. Talking about working conditions in American mills, for instance, he says, 'If properly improved, they will save us immense expence for the wages, provisions, cloathing, and lodging of workmen.'[6] Such an *if* signals not some hypothetical condition, but signals instead a real, and clear, political proposition. Dickens knew the power of such visionary, but attainable, *ifs*, and he used them often. He knew as well what a powerful responsibility the knowledge of an *if* imposes. When the reduced tradesman in *Oliver Twist* dies in a doorway at midnight from a 'want of the necessaries of life', the jury investigating the case begins to conclude that 'if the relieving officer had . . .' [OT.iv.21], but Bumble, who should have been that 'relieving officer', cuts them short. Society's Bumbles cannot stand the *if* as poser of possibility, since it places upon them the burden of making that *if* become an actuality.

The *if*, then, functions for the reader in very much the same way as the time telescope. It makes him aware of the possibilities of variety in human behaviour and response. Human beings make choices. They do not only react mechanically. They are capable of responding differently to the same situation, and it follows that since they do make choices, they must take responsibility for acting as they do.

> If [Mr Dorrit] had been a man with strength and purpose to face those troubles and fight them, he might have broken the net that held him [LD.I.vi.63].

> If Silas Wegg had been worse paid for his office, or better acquainted to discharge it, he would have considered these visits complimentary and agreeable [OMF.II.vii.296].

> If R. W. had been a more deserving object, she too might have condescended to come down from her pedestal for his beguilement [OMF.IV.v.679].

> Mrs Pardiggle would have got on infinitely better, if she had not had such a mechanical way of taking possession of people [BH.viii.107].

When Pip realises fully his ugly mistreatment of Joe, he cries heartily and thinks, 'If I had cried before, I should have had Joe with me then . . . . If I could have settled down, and been but half as fond of the forge as I was when I was little, I know it would have been much better for me' [GE.xvii.121].

While many of these *ifs* posit that a person would be different if his external environment were different – Mrs Wilfer would be more loving if her husband were more deserving – they also suggest that individuals could have responded differently – if they had only chosen to. And in fact Dickens's characters are forever asking themselves 'how should I respond if . . . ?' Monks wonders what would happen 'if I had only had the courage to say the word' and have Oliver killed [OT.xxxiii.217]. Amy Dorrit wonders what would happen 'if it could be' that her father were freed from prison [LD.I.ix.98–9]. What would happen, wonders Arthur Clennam, 'if [I] had the weakness to fall in love with Pet'? [LD.I.xvii.210] External circumstances do not necessarily determine character. Both Miss Wade and Esther Summerson are illegitimate daughters. But their responses to that situation are quite different. Both Dora Spenlow and Pet Meagles are made pets by their doting parents. But Pet grows up as Dora never does. Both Pancks and Wemmick face the same potentially dehumanising world of business. But their survival tactics are quite different. Choices and actions have consequences, and happy endings are caused and earned as well as freely given. What Dickens's *ifs* are often in the business of providing are ways and means of testing not only possible courses of action, but possible modes of response to the real world as well. Nell's grandfather says, 'If we are beggars–!' and Nell cuts him short. 'What if we are,' she says. 'Let us be beggars, and be happy!' [OCS.ix.71]

Joseph Wood Krutch even suggests of 'messier' writers like Shaw and Dickens that

we find them rich as sources of vicarious experiences and we find them interesting because their premises so closely resemble our own. The experiments which they suggest are experiments with which we ourselves are busy and the repertory of responses furnished by their characters is for us a more usable repertory than that afforded by the characters of Racine and Shakespeare.[7]

What *Hard Times* provides, for instance, is a repertory of responses to life in the real world, each one represented by a different character. One can try to classify, categorise, and ignore all that cannot be classified, as Gradgrind does before his change of heart. One can, like Bounderby, mindlessly seek to control all, and reduce all potential difficulty or complexity to 'turtle soup and venison and gold spoons'. One can stand aside and live life as the bemused spectator, as Harthouse does. And one can simply decline to live at all, and become an echoing spectre of others' responses, as Mrs Gradgrind does.

It would seem, though, that the ultimate virtue and the most highly recommended response to life in the novels is simply to endure and persevere. The list of those who do this in the novels is very long. Esther Summerson, Pa Wilfer, Amy Dorrit, Jenny Wren among the main characters, and countless hundreds on the peripheries, including Betty Higden, the Bagnets, Mr Jellyby and Caddy, the Plornishes, the Chiverys. Those who can be called 'happy' are rarely those who have most in the way of comfort and possessions. The Peggottys have very little. The Boffins are happy either with or without their money, and so are Bella Wilfer and John Harmon, who in effect earn their right to wealth and comfort by proving they can endure life without it. It takes Arthur Clennam the whole of the novel to find out what his proper response to life might be:

> 'But I like business,' says Pancks. 'What's a man made for?'
> 'For nothing else?' said Clennam.
> Pancks put the counter question, 'What else?' It packed up, in the smallest compass, a weight that had rested on Clennam's life, and he made no answer [LD.I.xiii.160].

Beyond all of these *ifs* which pose either potential for social change, or possibility for moral improvement, and beyond those that signal options or alternative responses for his characters, however, there is still another kind of *if* that signals something else: the presence of Fate, or accident. David Copperfield muses more than once that 'it would have been well for me (and for more than me), if I had had a steadfast and judicious father' [DC.xxii.322]. After Little Em'ly has run off with Steerforth, Ham muses: 'Odd times, I think if I hadn't had her promise for to marry me . . . she'd have told me what was struggling in her mind, and would have counselled with me, and I might have saved her' [DC.xl.737]. Harriet Carker wonders 'if she had remained with [her brother] the companion and friend she had been once, he might have escaped the crime into which he had fallen' [DS.liii.739].

These last two *ifs* would appear to be considerations of alternative courses of behaviour that might have been followed, and followed, preventative of disaster. But in fact these musings do not signal some real option characters had, for they could not in any instance *know* what was fated to happen, and all of their good intentions are finally irrelevant.

Sometimes, we and Dickens's characters can *see* the possibilities an *if* suggests, can see that changes are needed, can see that if this change is effected, this positive result will follow, but are powerless to bring about those changes. Of Plornish in *Little Dorrit*, a novel whose original title, significantly, was to have been 'Nobody's Fault', Dickens's narrator says:

> He could tell you who suffered, but he couldn't tell you whose fault it was. It wasn't *his* place to find out, and who'd mind what he said if he did find out? He only know'd that it wasn't put right by them what undertook that line of business, and that it didn't

come right of itself. And in brief his illogical opinion was that if
you couldn't do nothing for him, you had better take nothing
from him for doing of it [LD.I.xii.143].

Daniel Doyce invents some mysterious device that, if patented,
could help save England somehow. Or at least Mr Meagles believes
it would. But his propositions are endlessly circumnavigated by the
Government. The only *if* that Doyce can muster is hardly
conducive to action: 'If I don't complain,' he says, 'I can feel
gratitude' [LD.I.x.122–3]. The only *if* the narrator can muster is
equally frustrating. 'What a blessed thing it would have been for
him if he had taken a lesson in How not to do it' [LD.I.x.123]. Even
here Dickens throws on one more. 'Britannia herself might come to
look for lodgings in Bleeding Heart Yard, some ugly day or other, if
she over-did the Circumlocution Office': [LD.I.x.123]. If we cannot
effect change, we can at least threaten.

In spite of this last prophetic *if*, and in spite of the ominous
warnings to a stubborn and insensitive government, what is
fascinating about some of these *ifs* is that they sometimes look
toward a resignation of both responsibility and feeling. If things
cannot be improved, and must stay as they are, and if I am
powerless to change anything, then I'd just as soon not feel or know
it. It is this *if*, often an implied *if*, that sometimes rears its head.
Arthur Clennam muses:

He thought – who has not thought – that it might be better to flow
away monotonously, like the river, and to compound for its
insensibility to happiness with its insensibility to pain
[LD.I.xvi.200].

As Rogue Riderhood drifts in and out of consciousness after nearly
drowning, Dickens's narrator muses:

And yet – like us all, when we swoon – like us all, every day of our
lives when we wake – he is instinctively unwilling to be restored to
the consciousness of this existence, and would be left dormant, if
he could [OMF.III.iii.444–5].

It is the parenthetical matter that bothers: like all of us? who has not
thought? Where is the Dickens who wanted, or professed he wanted,
to show his readers that 'the world was not entirely to be despised'?

It would seem that here we have samples of that Dickens who carefully parcelled out his conflicting feelings, coming out strong in one direction only because he had the assurance of being able to come out strong in another as well.

But the simultaneous pull towards both feeling and action, insensibility and passivity, is not the only tension created in Dickens's novels by the word *if*. Dickens tried, as we know, to hold on to his beliefs in a moral universe, and to show that if people would behave morally and with foresight and consideration for their fellows, things would come out in the end. But the truth is that Dickens saw very well the part played simply by Fate or accident in determining the course of our lives. While it is true that Mr Brownlow adopts and protects Oliver Twist, it is chance or accident that saves Oliver as much as the good acts and intentions of Mr Brownlow. Oliver is almost signed over to the sadistic Gamfield to be used as a chimney sweep, and it is chance alone that saves him from this fate. The old gentleman who is to sign the papers happens to look up to find his inkwell, and in so doing he meets the eyes of the frightened child. The narrator muses, 'if the inkstand had been where the old gentleman thought it was' [OT.iii.18], Oliver's life would have progressed quite differently. Once Oliver runs away from Sowerberry the undertaker, it is Fate again that preserves him: 'If it hadn't been for a good-hearted Turnpikeman and a benevolent old lady, Oliver's troubles would have been shortened' [OT.viii.46].

The turnpikeman's benevolence, of course, is not caused by 'fate', but it is surely Oliver's luck and luck only that puts him in its path. He might just as easily have run into the thieving tinker with whom David Copperfield has to contend when *he* runs away. Goodness of heart saves Esther Summerson, Little Dorrit, and Arthur Clennam, but does very little for Magwitch, Stephen Blackpool, Betty Higden and Johnny. When Dickens recognises the unpredictability and pervasiveness of Fate in human affairs, and the inability of human beings to counteract it, he responds by retreating into the conditional.

It is not always or only Fate that intervenes to turn the *if* as possibility into the *if* as wistful might-have-been. Dickens wanted to change attitudes and feelings, but he was not always sure exactly how far he wanted to go, and whether he really wanted to change certain attitudes at all. He wanted to improve the lot of the working classes, but was appalled by labour organisers, whom he portrayed harshly in the person of Slackbridge in *Hard Times*, and by organised apprentices, whom he satirised in Sim Tappertit in *Barnaby Rudge*. When Dickens is feeling unsure or unclear as to exactly what attitude to hold toward a particular social problem, he often takes refuge in an evasionary *if*. Some of these are to be found at those occasions of social-sexual class-mixing which Dickens, as Taylor Stoehr shows, did feel uncomfortable with.[8] When Harry Maylie proposes to Rose, for instance, that proposal is couched in unending *ifs*:

> If your inclinations chime with your sense of duty . . . . If I had been less—less fortunate . . . If I could have done so, without doing heavy wrong to him I loved . . . If your lot had been differently cast . . . . If you had been even a little, but not so far above me; if I could have been a help and comfort to you in any humble scene of peace and retirement; and not a blot and drawback in ambitious and distinguished crowds . . . [OT.xxxv.261–2].

These *ifs* obviously posit not real possibilities for change, but are instead sighs and musings about that which 'cannot change'. Dickens solves the 'problem' of mixed-class marriage and Rose and Harry are married, not when he raises her to his station, but when he lowers himself to hers.

Among the possibilities that the *if* provides, then, is the possibility for evasion. Whether that evasion is couched in *if*, as here, or in the *seems*, as we saw earlier, it still constitutes a counter-statement to that of Dickens's confident moral rhetoric elsewhere. It admits of, and points to, incertitude. Once again, Dickens can be seen parcelling out his own conflicting attitudes. His Victorian optimism and faith in the possibilities of change the reader will find in his moral admonitions and assurances, and in some parts of his plots. But sometimes, in the simplest of words, he transmits to his readers his own incertitude as well.

6 The Dynamics of Description

Even in describing so palpable a thing as the slums of London, Dickens repeatedly insists upon the labyrinthine, maze-like confusion of the streets, courts and buildings, emphasising that quality of the district which makes its buildings seem indistinct as specific dwelling places and yet at the same time suggestive of dens and dungeons. The tottering and deserted hovels in which Fagin successively establishes his headquarters are all identical; they have no distinctive structure other than that, in almost surrealistic fashion, they are all single rooms reached by endless flights of stairs.[1]

Anyone who has ever seen David Lean's wonderful film of *Oliver Twist*, with its warrens and winding narrow streets through which urchins run like rats in the dark, has to know that no clear and simple Christian rhetoric can dispel that image of a confused and confusing world. There is a rhetoric of description, as critics from Charles Lamb, who talked about the 'dumb rhetoric of the scenery', to Robert Garis, who, describing Mrs Jellyby's house in *Bleak House*, concluded that 'every detail is a judgement' understood.[2] Even when we encounter what might appear to be simple, straight-forward description of person or place, because of Dickens's style of reportage, we can be fairly sure that it will begin to shade off immediately into something else: rhetorical admonition to social action or consciousness, or an invitation to escape into a world of fantasy.

In a way, then, if everything in Dickens's novels has rhetorical content, everything in Dickens's novels is also description, and could be talked about as such. Here is a passage of description of Tom-all-Alone's in *Bleak House*:

It is a black, dilapidated street, avoided by all decent people; where the crazy houses were seized upon, when their decay was far advanced, by some bold vagrants, who, after establishing their own possession, took to letting them out in lodgings. Now, these tumbling tenements contain, by night, a swarm of misery. As, on the ruined human wretch, vermin parasites appear, so these ruined shelters have bred a crowd of foul existence that crawls in and out of gaps in walls and boards; and coils itself to sleep, in maggot numbers, where the rain drips in; and comes and goes, fetching and carrying fever, and sowing more evil in its every foot-print than Lord Coodle, and Sir Thomas Doodle, and the Duke of Foodle, and all the fine gentlemen in office, down to Zoodle, shall set right in five hundred years – though born expressly to do it.

Twice, lately, there has been a crash and a cloud of dust, like the springing of a mine, in Tom-all-Alone's; and each time, a house has fallen. These accidents have made a paragraph in the newspapers, and have filled a bed or two in the nearest hospital. The gaps remain, and there are not unpopular lodgings among the rubbish. As several more houses are nearly ready to go, the next crash in Tom-all-Alone's may be expected to be a good one.

This desirable property is in Chancery, of course. It would be an insult to the discernment of any man with half an eye, to tell him so. Whater 'Tom' is the popular representative of the original plaintiff in Jarndyce and Jarndyce; or whether Tom lived here when the suit had laid the street waste, all alone, until other settlers came to join him; or whether the traditional title is a comprehensive name for a retreat cut off from honest company and put out of the pale of hope; perhaps nobody knows [BH.xvi.220].

It is easy enough to see how impossible it is ever to extricate description from all that goes with it in Dickens's prose. In the first sentence of this passage, the first half of the sentence is pure description; the second half shades off into editorial comment. The first half of the first paragraph is primarily vivid description; the second half is political commentary. The second paragraph is an example of what I have earlier called 'time-telescoping', in which Dickens tells his readers what Tom-all-Alone's is now, what it used to be in the past, what caused its decline, and finally, what is going to happen to it in the future, in a bit of that Dickensian prophecy that is signalled by the word *if*. The metaphors in the passage are all essentially rhetorical in function, full of moral judgement and social indictment. They are what I. A. Richards would call 'semi-surreptitious' metaphors; occasions for the writer to 'smuggle in' commentary under the guise of description.[3] As often as not, Dickens's descriptions are also full of what Richards would call 'projectile adjectives', as people pass along 'villainous streets', and by 'infamous courts', feeling 'as if [they] were going every moment deeper down, into the infernal gulf' [BH.xxii.310].[4] As the description continues, Dickens's words become more and more fantastical. It is almost as if the place itself is so horrible that it cannot be approximated except by triangulation, and the points from which we do that triangulating are always fantastical, because only there are there terms adequate to describing the experience of Tom-all-Alone's. The last paragraph of this description provides another example of one of the staples of Dickensian description. Here the narrator, so far so conscientious in his description, no longer assumes the stance of omniscience at all, but confesses instead real bewilderment as to what is or is not true. This is the authorial bewilderment in the midst of rhetorical commentary I have described elsewhere.

One feature and effect of Dickens's descriptions we have not yet talked about, however, and it is to my mind one of the most significant. In spite of the fact that Dickens's descriptions brim over with specific details, as often as not those details are never integrated into either a coherent pattern or a clear visual picture of a locale at all. We see and hear only what the participants in the action see and hear. At the beginning of *Little Dorrit*, for instance, the reader sits in the prison cell with Cavalletto and Rigaud, registering sensations exactly as they do, and from their vantage point. Or, more precisely, from their hearing point: 'The noise of the key in the lock arrested them both. The sound of voices succeeded, and the tread of feet. The door clashes, the voices and the feet came on, and the prison-keeper slowly ascended the stairs' [LD.I.i.12]. In the same way is the scene described as Oliver is lowered into a house to rob it, and then shot. There is little difficulty in determining where the 'immediacy' of Dickens's prose comes after reading such scenes as that one:

The cry was repeated – a light appeared – a vision of two terrified half-dressed men at the top of the stairs swam before his eyes – a flash – a loud noise – a smoke – a crash somewhere, but where he knew not, – and he staggered back. . . . Then came the loud ringing of a bell: mingled with the noise of fire-arms, and the shouts of men, and the sensation of being carried over uneven ground at a rapid pace. And then, the noises grew confused in the distance; and a cold deadly feeling crept over the boy's heart; and he saw or heard no more [OT.xxii.163–4].

But a scene in which many details are presented, and presented only from the vantage point of a person in the midst of the action, effects much more than simply a feeling of immediacy. William Harvey is one of those critics who have talked about the way the massive amount of detail Dickens uses is the sign of a 'primitive, animistic imagination'. Dickens believed – really believed, says Harvey – that objects are not just ' "out there", opaque, other-than-us', but also 'alive, hostile, benevolent'.[5] But Dickens's use of all of this detail, his attempts to describe everything, can be seen as primitive in another and equally significant way. What the primitive does when he names a thing, whether by freezing its image in stone or wood or capturing it in words, is in some way to gain control over that object: 'This I have touched and named, and therefore am master over it.' Dickens lived at a time in which men felt particularly fearful of the increasingly mechanised civilisation they saw around them. His theme, according to Donald Fanger, was 'the great modern city . . . whose transformation was going on before [his] eyes, signalling the end of "nature" and the "natural life", and the beginning of "modernity".'[6] We could, then, just as easily see Dickens's impulse to name everything, to collect all of the details surrounding a scene and present them to us complete, as an attempt to 'freeze' the world; to stop the process of transformation for a moment so that the pattern and coherence of the world might be more readily apparent. If he names everything, describes everything, then the pattern will become clear, and he – and his readers – will be able to really *see*. But it is, I think, out of the disappointment of his and our expectation that a part of Dickens's impact comes, because, of course, totality of description or accuracy of detail never result in a very effective representation of the objects being described. Objects tend to resist our attempts to pattern them. They remain stubbornly what they are.

When David Copperfield and Mr Peggotty travel to Westminster to try to find Martha Endell, who has been both literally and morally 'lost' in the city, both David and Mr Peggotty scan the city for clues as to why she went there at all. But the details accumulated and presented provide no real clues and certainly provide no answers:

> There were neither wharves nor houses on the melancholy waste of road near the great blank Prison. A sluggish ditch deposited its mud at the prison walls. Coarse grass and rank weeds straggled over all the marshy land in the vicinity. In one part, carcases of houses, inauspiciously begun and never finished, rotted away. In another, the ground was cumbered with rusty iron monsters of steam-boilers, wheels, cranks, pipes, furnaces, paddles, anchors, diving bells, windmill-sails, and I know not what strange objects, accumulated by some speculator, and grovelling in the dust, underneath which – having sunk into the soil of their own weight in wet weather – they had the appearance of vainly trying to hide themselves [DC.xlvii.679–80].

This description looks uncannily like that which Faulkner provides in *Light in August*, in which what is described in a field is a spot where there are

> . . . gaunt, staring, motionless wheels rising from mounds of brick and rubble and ragged weeds with a quality profoundly astonishing, and gutted boilers lifting their rusting and unsmoking stacks with an air stubborn, baffled and bemused upon a stumppocked scene of profound and peaceful desolation, unploughed, untilled, gutting slowly into red and choked ravines.[7]

The similarity should hardly surprise us. Both writers were watching an old order in the process of transforming into something new and other. Both describe scenes in which man's hand has been heavy in destroying the natural, and converting it into what is now little more than rubble. The old graces and beauties – whether they be the beauties of an aristocratic, agrarian South, or of an Early Victorian England – are rapidly disappearing. What remains of old mansions are for both writers now no more than 'carcases'. And the new order was still powerless to be born. What has replaced the old order, so far as either Dickens or Faulkner can see, is rubble, and time and time again they scan the rubble for clues that will help them – and us – perceive the shape and pattern and direction of the new order. But as the observer scans this scene, we find nothing much to suggest that new order at all. We can accumulate details for ever, attribute to objects sentience and purpose (in Dickens's description objects try to hide themselves; in Faulkner's the gutted boilers themselves survey the field in which they lie), but the objects can tell us nothing – and not even, at times, their own function – no matter how systematically or carefully we survey them. Objects described in great profusion do not simplify the business of seeing: they complicate it. Each detail contains a promise of pattern and revelation, and a threat of irrelevance.

It is not merely that all of these objects have a life and a personality of their own, although that is true as often as not. Beyond this, to understand the effects of a Dickensian superfluity of detail, one must understand something of the nature of perception. In his book *Visual Thinking* Rudolf Arnheim describes perception not as a passive recording of stimulus material, but as a much more active concern of the mind. We do not simply register details and then total them up to arrive at a 'picture'. Instead, our senses operate selectively. Perception, then, is very much a problem-solving activity: which of all that assaults my senses shall I pay attention to, and which shall I ignore?[8] Insofar as Dickens's reader must occupy himself in the same kind of selectivity process at every point at which Dickens describes anything, Dickens's novels force the reader to duplicate this same experience of perception.

The tenth chapter of *Bleak House* is called 'The Law-writer', and begins, significantly, not with the law-writer at all, but with a discussion and description of Snagsby:

On the eastern borders of Chancery Lane, that is to say, more particularly in Cook's Court, Cursitor Street, Mr Snagsby, Law-Stationer, pursues his lawful calling. In the shade of Cook's Court, at most times a shady place, Mr Snagsby has dealt in all sorts of blank forms of legal process; in skins and rolls of parchment; in paper – foolscap, brief, draft, brown, white, whitey-brown, and blotting; in stamps; in office-quills, pens, ink, India-rubber, pounce, pins, pencils, sealing-wax, and wafers; in red tape and green ferret; in pocket-books, almanacks, diaries, and law lists; in string boxes, rulers, inkstands – glass and leaden, pen-knives, scissors, bodkins, and other small office-cutlery; in short, in articles too numerous to mention [BH.x.127].

The comedy is of various kinds. The narrator, for one thing, is another Micawber. For another, he tells us of things too numerous to mention, but mentions them all. For another, Dickens's private joke is that he is getting paid to do all this: filling up yet another monthly part of his novel with such catalogues as this. But the accumulation of detail does other things too. Among other things, it is diversionary. For the *subject* of this chapter – insofar as the plot is concerned – is a meeting between Mr Tulkinghorn and Mr Snagsby, the end result of which is that Tulkinghorn will determine the identity of the law-writer whose handwriting has so disturbed the composure of Lady Dedlock. And the direct result of that discovery will be the death of Lady Dedlock. But before we can follow that plot line, we must wade our way through an extra-ordinary amount of detail, of which the above is only the smallest sample. Not only are we given the catalogue of items above, but immediately following, the details – both a physical description and a past history – of the sign 'Peffer and Snagsby' that hangs outside the law-stationer's office. And then details surrounding the past history of Peffer himself, now deceased. And details as to where he is buried. And then the story of Peffer's niece and her upbringing, and of her marriage to Snagsby. And then details of Snagsby's marital troubles. And then details of the history of Guster, the Snagsbys' serving girl. One could go on. And Dickens does. The point is that Dickens sets up a veritable fog of detail between his readers and his plot. After pages of detail on the Snagsbys, their house, their neighbourhood, their servant, our attention is finally directed across Chancery Lane and Court and Lincoln's Inn Garden, and into Lincoln's Inn Fields, there to meet the second person of importance in the scene, Mr Tulkinghorn. Yet, here, too, we must wade our way through an overwhelming collection of detail, and a miscellany much like that surrounding Snagsby:

> Here, in a large house, formerly a house of state, lives Mr Tulkinghorn. It is let off in sets of chambers now; and in those shrunken fragments of its greatness, lawyers lie like maggots in nuts. But its roomy staircases, passages, and ante-chambers still remain; and even its painted ceilings, where Allegory, in Roman helmet and celestial linen, sprawls among balustrades and pillars, flowers, clouds, and big-legged boys, and makes the head ache – as would seem to be Allegory's object always, more or

less. Here, among his many boxes labelled with transcendent names, lives Mr Tulkinghorn [BH.x.130].

But even such distractions as a description of Mr Tulkinghorn's ceiling do not end the flood of detail. Only after another full page does Mr Tulkinghorn finally leave his office and make his way to Snagsby's and even here we must learn first more details of Snagsby's life and habits before the meeting finally takes place, learning, among other things, at what hours the Snagsbys have tea and dinner, the fact that Guster's hair won't grow, and which smells hover in the air at this particular time of day.

One way to talk about the way detail functions in the novels is to talk about field and ground. To a large extent there is no background or foreground in Dickens's world. All things reside on the same flat plane, and nothing recedes into the background until the reader puts it there. Focus, insofar as there is any, is that which the reader provides. On the occasion on which Jarvis Lorry first meets Lucie Manette to tell her of her father's release from prison, for instance, he has difficulty even seeing her amidst the miscellaneous objects in the dim room:

> The obscurity was so difficult to penetrate that Mr Lorry, picking his way over the well-worn Turkey carpet, supposed Miss Manette to be, for the moment, in some adjacent room, until, having got past the two tall candles, he saw standing . . . a young lady [TTC.I.iv.18].

Sometimes objects clarify rather than confuse or complicate. Podsnap's furniture or the Veneerings' possessions simply reflect their ponderousness and ostentation. But at other times, 'things' simply confuse.

This is not to say, however, that Dickens's art was somehow 'flawed'. Insofar as Dickens's fiction is full of miscellaneous concrete detail given to the reader in no necessarily coherent order, what that description does is set the reader down in the midst of a teeming world. This mode of presentation in no sense constitutes a 'report' of some action that happened in the past. It is instead a recreation of an experience or an event, with the one important difference that the reader has been invited – or rather, has been thrust – into the midst of the scene to make sense of it for himself. George Orwell was right when he called Dickens 'all fragments, all details'.[9] But this is hardly a defect. Each of us provides his own patterning out of what Dickens describes time and again as the 'dimly perceptible'. Dickens's novels, then, must be seen as providing not only a 'vision' – of the power of love, for instance – but also as providing the raw materials from which we can construct our own vision. I would suspect that each of us selects from those raw materials, that wealth of incident and detail, his own vision, and this is another part of the reason why opinions as to whether Dickens was finally and ultimately a 'dark' or a 'comic' writer, an optimist or a pessimist, vary. Some of us choose to focus on the plots and their happy resolution for the main characters in the novels. Some of us may choose to regard – or cannot help regarding – Dickens's descriptions of a confusing and bewildering London with its noises, jostling people and buildings in the process of transforming, as more a real place than simply a setting in which his characters play out their assigned roles. Both of these experiences of the Dickens world are valid, and ultimately each reader pays his money and takes his choice. In many a reader of the novels, I would suspect that the final feeling is that both visions are there, and that both are equally compelling. Dickens's confident moral and social rhetorical interventions into his novels lead us to believe that we are being comfortably led to a singular vision. But in spite of the rhetorical directions and the neat resolutions of plot, Dickens's world remains – insofar as we see it dissolved in description – multiple and confusing. To put Dickens's descriptive world back together with his frequent rhetorical admonitions that we open our eyes and see, is to discover that Dickens's style both demands, with urgency, that we see, while at the same time thwarting our attempts at even the simplest seeing.

2 DESCRIPTION AS DEFENCE

He saved himself from the despair of the dream in *The Chimes* by taking the world for granted and busying himself with its details.[1]

To overwhelm the senses with detail as Dickens does is to insure that some of that detail will be only half-seen, that some will be missed altogether, and that some will be absorbed and perceived only long after its initial registering on our senses. Dickens seems to have been aware that his superfluity of detail could at times operate defensively, protecting his reader from the potentially discomfiting parts of his vision. Fagin focuses on details of the architecture of the courtroom so that he won't have to focus on the fact of his own impending death:

> Even while he trembled, and turned burning hot at the idea of speedy death, he fell to counting the iron spikes before him, and wondering how the head of one had been broken off, and whether they would mend it, or leave it as it was [OT.lii.405].

When David Copperfield first meets and has to call Murdstone 'father', he goes off to his room alone to try to accept that unpleasant reality, but the most he can do is focus on bits and piece of his room:

> I thought of the oddest things. Of the shape of the room, of the cracks in the ceiling, of the paper on the wall, of the flaws in the window glass making ripples and dimples on the prospect, of the washing-stand being ricketty on its three legs [DC.iv.44].

In the same way that Dickens's characters sometimes focus on details to spare themselves pain, sometimes Dickens focuses his readers' attention on details for the same reason, and precisely at those moments when some incident of great importance is happening, we are not there to see it. We come on the scene only *after* Krook's spontaneous combustion; only *after* Little Nell has died. (It has always seemed curious to me that *The Old Curiosity Shop* is most remembered for a death scene that isn't even there.)

What can we say about the effects of such a mode of description? Most simply, it demonstrates that Dickens could provide quite enough emotional content to impress a scene on his readers' minds and hearts without necessarily allowing them to 'see' it at all. His rhetorical interventions, full of projectile adjectives (*splendid, glorious, ugly, horrid, lovely, pretty*); his complete and careful catalogue of the sounds, sights, smells, surrounding and subsequent to an event served well enough to make the reader feel he had really 'been there' when in fact he had not. One has, then, all of the advantages of emotional participation in the scene, but without having to endure any of the more unseemly details of the actual event. Like Nell's grandfather, we can tiptoe into the room only after the event, to see 'her couch, dressed with here and there some winter berries and green leaves . . .' [OCS.lxxi.538–9].

Sikes's murder of Nancy is most vivid, and we are there to see it happen, blow by blow. But the murder of the Marquis in *A Tale of Two Cities* is one of those off-stage events. Dickens begins by directing our attention to the night itself: its sounds, smells and atmosphere. He follows by directing our attention to the stables outside the Marquis's château. Then describes the village. Then the burial ground outside the château. Then the sun rising is described. We see and hear the village awaken, and later hear and see life beginning to stir in the château. But what we learn at the end of all this careful catalogue is that while our attention had been focused there, on all the details, the Marquis had been murdered in his bed [TTC.II.ix. 120–2]. This scene and all others like it in Dickens must engender in the reader the feeling that the world is so very large, and that so much happens in any given hour, that while our attention is focused in one place, it is drawn there more arbitrarily than not, and other events, no less important than those we pay attention to now, are happening elsewhere. In this way and for this reason, then, Dickens's novels feel busy and rich. They are always at least potentially about worlds and events outside themselves; about what is *not* there, as well as about what is. *Our Mutual Friend*, though a good novel, is not so good as others of Dickens's novels in part because in that novel nearly everything happens 'on-stage', and that sense of a rich world beyond our ken is missing. The Lammles, the Rokesmiths, Eugene Wrayburn and Lizzie Hexam marry on-stage; Riderhood, Bradley Headstone, Mr Dolls, all die there. It may well be that because nothing seems to be happening outside our line of vision, we are less interested in what is happening inside it. In the best of Dickens's novels, his habit of making the reader feel that there are other events and other lives outside our range of vision, his practice of splitting our attention between one scene or world and another, comes very close to re-creating, again, the experience of trying to make sense out of life. As in life, there are choices to be made, decisions as to what we see and what we ignore. As in life, there are events we will miss because we were paying attention to something else we thought was important. If Dickens is to be called 'realistic', his realism might best be regarded as a kind of emotional realism: a fidelity to our own notions of what it feels like to be a conscious human being. Fagin's keen attention to everything in the courtroom at the moment of his sentencing provides him with a protective defence against one kind of reality, while at the same time assuring him that he is alive by providing him with another reality. The contemporary inheritor of this practice is Joyce Carol Oates whose characters inevitably pay attention in some dreamy way to the tiles on the floor, or shadows on the wall, or anything other than the world around them: Elena Howe in *Do with me What you Will*; Richard Everett in *Expensive People*.

David Copperfield's vivid remembrances of the smell of fog, the sight of hoar frost, the feel of his own rimy black hair, and the sound of boys at school tapping their feet and blowing on their chilled fingers, constitute his whole knowledge of his mother's death – a death he had not been present at. Like Fagin or David, most of us remember our past and our lives by means of the significant – and often the insignificant – detail. So do most of us protect ourselves from more unpleasant realities by concentrating on more pleasant – or at least less threatening – ones. Dickens's novels, because of his use of defensive description, focus our attention on both kinds of reality. Dickens has two descriptive modes of presentation, one confrontive and one evasive; one directs our gaze to the physical and existential sufferings in the world around us, and the other leads it away. The predominant confrontive mode leads the reader to expect that everything, not only the relevant but the irrelevant, will be described for him. But the expectations generated by this mode are sometimes thwarted by the presence of the evasive mode, and the reader's response to the Dickens world is richer because this is so.

3 DESCRIPTIONS AND REPETITIONS

Repetition creates a feeling that some kind of order, logic, purposefulness, plan, cause, or pattern is being imposed on content.[1]

An idea never halts, never repeats itself. It must be changing every moment, for to cease to change would be to cease to live. Let gesture display a like animation! Let it accept the fundamental law of life, which is the complete negation of repetition.[2]

In *Structuralist Poetics*, Jonathan Culler notes that 'to say that there is a great deal of parallelism and repetition in literary texts is of little interest in itself and of less explanatory value. The crucial question is what effects patterning can have, and one cannot', he says, 'approach an answer unless one incorporates within one's theory an account of how readers take up and structure elements of a text.'[3] Culler is using the word *repetition* here to refer to any recurrence – of image, sequence, for instance – but I should like to suggest that what he says is true of repetitions of the simplest and most literal kind: repetitions of phrase, gesture in characters in a novel. What do repetitions do to readers of Dickens's texts, and how might readers pattern them?

A great many of Dickens's novels begin with repetitions, of course. In *Our Mutual Friend* and *Dombey and Son*, as well as in *Bleak House*, the syntactical parallelisms form a kind of rhythm, lulling the reader and easing him into the novel. In other novels, *Little Dorrit*, for instance, the repetition of the word *staring* functions in the same way, 'lulling the imagination, rocking it to and fro . . . and thus preparing it submissively to accept the vision suggested'.[4] Since, as I have said, Dickens's world is one in which the reader will encounter not only a bright vision, but hordes of starving children and abused paupers as well, and since such sights need to be, in Simon Lesser's words, 'walled off from the world of experience'[5] by an artistic frame, we might assume that these initial repetitions were Dickens's way of leading his readers 'painlessly' into a world where he was very likely to find not only much warmth and comedy, but much pain, references to social injustice, and, on the peripheries, much moral evil as well.

Repetition is, of course, also one of the staples of Dickensian comedy. Whenever Dickens needed a sure laugh, he created another character who, whenever he or she came on-stage, performed some comic gesture – banged his head against walls, winked, blinked, or harumphed – or repeated some phrase with reasonable regularity – 'not to deceive you', 'Barkis is willin' – giving the reader still another pleasant moment.

In the shifting, transforming world Dickens creates, however, repetition serves yet another and more important function. We all know that instinctively we arm ourselves to meet the unknown by repeating the known; what we *do* have of the fixed, the final, the true, the predictable. Dickens arms us in the same way as we wander through the world he creates. Thus, whatever else may happen in *David Copperfield*, we know that Barkis will always be willin'. Whatever strange and grotesque people accost David on the highways, he knows that Mrs Micawber will never leave Mr

Micawber, and that Mrs Gummidge can be expected to go through periodic 'lone lorn creetur' phases, and will come be comforted by the Peggottys when things 'go contrary' with her. Krook may spontaneously combust, but Miss Flite will always carry her reticule. Whatever mysteries, strange sounds and strange visitors pervade and invade the Clennam house in *Little Dorrit*, we can be sure that Affrey will always respond to them in the same way, by throwing her apron over her head. Repeated gestures and phrases, then, provide the reader with security, predictability, continuity, assurances that what is, always will be. Such predictability constitutes a perfect counter-statement to that made by Dickens's peripheral and imagic worlds, both of which are, as I have said, quite other than predictable.

For the characters themselves, repetition often serves as another kind of reassurance or comfort. In *The Psychoanalytic Theory of Neurosis* Otto Fenichel says 'the psychological function of play is to get rid of . . . tensions by the active repetition or anticipation of them in a self-chosen time'.[6] So when Micawber repeats over and over again that something will 'turn up', his words are really a kind of play aimed at providing him with assurance and comfort, something that David Copperfield recognises with chagrin each time he has taken one of Micawber's suicide notes at face value, only to discover later that Micawber's *expression* of his suffering has in fact relieved that suffering.[7] Joe Gargery's repetitions of 'such larks!' at the bedside of Pip are his assurance – to himself and to Pip – that he and Pip will, in spite of illness, upheaval, estrangements of all kinds, be able to return to the forge and fields together. When Cap'n Cuttle thinks that Walter Gay was been drowned, his repetitions of 'Poor Wal'r, Drownded an't he?' [DS.xlix,682,683,684,687,688] are meant to console Florence, and curiously enough they do have that effect. Toots, hopelessly in love with Florence, consoles himself by repeating over and over again, 'It's of no consequence.'

Repetition of phrase or gesture, or of phrase become gesture can be seen, then, as the action of people at play, entertaining either themselves and us and each other with their repetitions, or finding relief from suffering through its articulation and repetition.

But the reader who consults his own responses to Dickens's characters will discover that not all of them, and not all of their repeated phrases and gestures, are equally funny, equally comforting, or equally reassuring. If Dickens was, as he surely was, interested in bringing about a 'change of heart' in human beings and in awakening people's sensibilities to and sense of responsibility for the poor, then nothing could be more hopeless and more surely counter-indicated than characters moving and speaking in entirely predictable and unchanging ways. Bounderby in *Hard Times* endlessly repeats the story of his 'impoverished' childhood (it is a lie, we discover late in the novel), and endlessly repeats his analysis of the state of the workers in Coketown: they all want 'to be fed on turtle soup and venison with a gold spoon'. But Bounderby is not particularly funny; is more odious than funny. And he is not funny because what he represents and calls up are all those people who cannot see, cannot perceive, cannot hear and cannot change; who can only go round and round in the same groove, endlessly repeating the same story. Bounderby is even more unfunny in his repetitions because he has the power to inflict his monotony and his imperceptions on others; represents not only inflexibility, but inflexibility combined with power. Henri Bergson says that society cannot survive if its members have rigidities and inelasticities, and that laughter often functions as society's way of expressing its displeasure at

> inelasticity of character, of mind, and even of body, because it is the possible sign of a slumbering activity, as well as of an activity with separatist tendencies. Society needs its members aiming after an increasingly delicate adjustment of wills which will fit more and more perfectly into one another.[8]

So Bounderby, or Dombey, who with rigid back repeatedly rolls the words 'Dom-bey and Son' off his tongue, or Sir Leicester Dedlock, who endlessly repeats his analysis of how England is headed for doom because the aristocracy is no longer secure in its power, are not really 'funny'. If we laugh at them, our laugh is what Bergson suggests: a kind of 'social gesture' that expresses both our discomfort with and our disapproval of such rigidity. Mrs Gummidge may repeat her 'lone lorn creetur' analysis over and over, but in Mr Peggotty's pain and distress at losing Little Em'ly she *can* alter her responses, and she does. When Peggotty discovers that Little Em'ly has run off with Steerforth, she cries out, 'Oh my lone, lorn Dan'l . . . what have *my* contrairies ever been to this!' [DC.xxxi.454] David Copperfield is astounded at this change, and it is Dickens speaking as well as David, saying, 'I could not meditate

enough upon the lesson that I read in Mrs Gummidge'
[DC.xxxii.459]. The lesson is that which Bergson talks about.
Repetition that does not respond to our sanctioning laughter by
altering itself is not funny, or is funny only initially and until we
comprehend exactly what such inelasticity and rigidity implies. In
his book *Telling it Again and Again*, Bruce Kawin distinguishes
between what is 'repetitious', and what is 'repetitive'. His distinctions are arbitrary, of course – I would be inclined to reverse them –
but nonetheless his point is that what is 'repetitious' loses
power with each recurrence; is enervating. What is 'repetitive'
gathers force and impact with each recurrence.[9] In Dickens's
novels, some repetitions nourish; others disturb.

If the repeated phrase of one character can be either comforting or disturbing, so too can the repeated physical gesture.
Consider a handful of the repeated gestures we meet in several
novels: Magwitch's hugging himself in times of stress; Mr Merdle's
taking himself in custody with his own hands; Mr Jellyby's banging
his head against walls; Uriah Heep's wringing his hands; and
Pecksniff's 'moral' tears that ooze out of his eyes whenever he
suspects that they might ingratiate him with someone who could
give him money. Magwitch hugs himself when times are rough. To
the reader, this entirely unconscious and spontaneous gesture must
seem and feel entirely human and right. Having no parents, being
his own protector almost since birth, it seems natural that he should
hug himself in times of stress. Mr Merdle's taking himself into
custody we are not so sure of. Surely it is a bit less a 'natural' gesture,
and a bit more a sign of the stirrings of guilt or of psychological
disturbance. The same can be said for Jaggers's constant washing of
his hands after an encounter with a client, which the Leavises liken
to the hand-washing of Pontius Pilate.[10] As we move down the
range of repeated gestures from Jaggers's to Uriah Heep's 'umble
wringing of hands, however, we begin to suspect that there are
major differences between one and the other. Uriah Heep's
wringing of hands may be a natural, unconscious gesture. But our
strong suspicion is that it is not, and it is in its contrivedness that it is
so distasteful. Surely when we come to Pecksniff's tears, completely
artificial and not at all 'natural', we not only laugh, but find the
character quite odious. 'A comic character is comic', says Bergson,
'in proportion to his ignorance of himself. . . . He becomes invisible
to himself while remaining visible to all the world.'[11] The charm of
Magwitch's gesture is that it is so natural and unconscious. Pecksniff

and Uriah Heep cease to be funny at precisely that moment at which the reader becomes aware that *they* are aware of their own gestures, and using them to gain favour with their fellows by connivance or contrivance. Simon Tappertit, Pecksniff, Podsnap and Heep are odious because they are conscious of their contrived gestures, and funny only because and insofar as they are unconscious of the *real* (as opposed to the assumed) effect of their gesture.

There is, however, a whole further range of repeated gestures and phrases that are capable of causing different responses in readers. If the Victorians – or any of us, really – take some comfort in the expected and the predictable in a world full of change, they and we also fear the kind of repeated gesture that suggests man-turned-machine. Flintwinch, 'like some eccentric mechanical force' [LD.I.xxix.339], periodically 'makes springs' after Affery [LD.I.xxix.340], very much like a machine. Very much, in fact, like Sloppy's mangle that threatens to leap after the 'minders' in Betty Higden's hovel. When we discover that he can drink great quantities of alcohol and stay quite sober, we are even more sure that he is really a machine. And that may have been, to the Victorians who were already awed by and fearful of the machine, a very disconcerting feeling.[12] The abrupt repetitions of Mr F's Aunt in *Little Dorrit* are enough to make the reader feel that she, too, is somewhat akin to one of the more clattering Victorian machines gone mad and unpredictable. She may be less wilful – less sane – than Flintwinch, but she is just as frightening.

The human-being-turned-mechanical was more than a metaphor for Dickens, and more than a joke. What man who signalled by phrase or gesture that he had become machine meant to Dickens and the Victorians was that he had become incapable not only of change, but of feeling. Mrs General, the model of deportment from whom Amy Dorrit is supposed to learn how to be a 'lady', has a manner that is 'perfect, considered as a piece of machinery' [LD.II.i.435]. Pancks has 'no tastes or inclinations'. He knows nothing but work. 'Keep me at it,' he says [LD.I.xiii.160].

But Pancks turns out, in spite of his apparent mechanical nature, to be human as well. So does Bradley Headstone, who, though he does everything 'mechanically', [OMF.II.i.217] has a superfluity of human passion as well. At this point one must admit to something very much like an ambiguous response to many of Dickens's characters and their repeated gestures and phrases. We do not see them as merely amusing, or as merely mechanical. In fact, we become unsure of *what* to make of them. The line between the reassuring repetition and the disturbing repetition is at best very fine, and at worst very hazy. Do we find comfort, for instance, in Mrs Joe Gargery's ritualistic and mechanical cutting of bread slices for Pip and Joe? Is it a human act – getting pins stuck in the bread slices as she shoves them up against her apron-front to cut them, and neither noticing it nor caring, nor changing her way of cutting the bread – or is it a mechanical act? Increasingly, we meet in Dickens's world real people having to contend with machines disguised as people, or having to try to discover which *are* people, and which machines.

Mr Chuffey in *Martin Chuzzlewit* seems to be a machine. He sits every evening by the fireside and is never seen to speak or move, except when 'a cup of tea was given him, in which he was seen to soak his bread mechanically. There was no reason to suppose that he went to sleep at these seasons, or that he heard, or saw, or felt, or thought. He remained, as it were, frozen up' [MC.xi.182]. Has Dickens here created another comic character, or is Chuffey one of those Dickensian machines masquerading as a human being, or are there haunting traces here of our own fears made concrete; the fear that the pains of existence – or a long career as an accountant – will make us, too, 'mechanical', and 'frozen up'? What are we to make of the endlessly repeated court routine of Miss Flite? To see her endlessly repeated routine as representative of people's human, if silly, habit of repeating futile gestures as comic because predictable, or as funny because mechanical, is to see a comic vision and a comic Dickens. But to see Miss Flite's endlessly repeated routine as representative of people's repetitions of futile gestures in the face of that over which they have no control is to see a dark vision and a dark Dickens. I would suspect that most readers, whether they are aware of doing so or not, tend to hover somewhere between the two extremes, feeling ambiguously about these repetitions and what they represent.

Repetition, which on the simplest level is suggestive of re-assurance, humanness and comedy, moves not only to the more ambiguous and less comic realm of man-become-machine, but finally shades off into realms that are still more disconcerting. Miss Havisham goes round and round her dusty wedding table quietly repeating

> Old Clem! With a thump and a sound –
> Old Clem! Beat it out, beat it out –
> Old Clem! . . . [GE.xii.89],

and Mrs Clennam endlessly rocks by the fire in her chair, but surely the reader finds nothing comforting in these repetitions. In them, Dickens has embodied the Victorian – or ageless – fear of stasis or sameness; has led us by stages to the realm of the repetition without contrast; has created the realm of what might be called the violently static.[13] 'I know nothing of the days of the week; I know nothing of weeks of the year' [GE.viii.56] Miss Havisham tells Pip. Mrs Clennam, who is described like Chuffey, as 'frozen up', says, 'all seasons are alike to me . . . . I know nothing of summer and winter, shut up here' [LD.I.iii.34]. In more pleasant circumstances, time is measured off in and by the reappearance of expected repetitions: in *Oliver Twist*, by the daily rising of the sun that temporarily erases for Oliver the terrors of the night [OT.xlviii.323]; in *Our Mutual Friend*, by the daily reappearance at her door of Mrs Wilfer in her gloves and scarf; and in *David Copperfield* by the nightly reappearance of Mr Peggotty's lantern in the window to light the way home for Em'ly.

If there is no repetition, if there is no alternation between one condition and another, then how is one to feel anything at all?[14] Time passes with reference to the senses, not to a clock. We feel vaguely disconcerted by John Willett and his cronies in *Barnaby Rudge* who doze away the years refusing to acknowledge time and change. What is frightening about the Dedlocks' homes in Lincolnshire and Lincoln's Inn Hall is that they are places pretty much like Miss Havisham's room or Mrs Clennam's house; places outside of time and immune to sensation. When Dickens's narrator describes the view from Lady Dedlock's window as 'alternately a lead-coloured view and a view in Indian ink' [BH.ii.9], with damp grounds outside in which 'the soft loppings and prunings of the woodman's axe can make no crash or crackle as they fall' [BH.ii.8], Dickens has conjured up those images that would be part of a Victorian nightmare, in which senses no longer register sights and sounds, and contrasts no longer exist, and change is no longer possible or to be hoped for. The worst of homes in Dickens's novels seem to shut out all sensation (a curious phenomenon, and perhaps productive of ambiguity as well, for the *best* of homes also do the same thing). The Clennam home makes Affery feel 'as if she were deaf' [LD.I.xv.178], since sounds from the street seem to rush by without stopping. The Casbys' house, too, is a 'sober, silent, air-tight house . . . and the door, closing again, seem[s] to shut out sound and motion' [LD.I.xiii.145].

To Dickens, who wore vests brilliantly embroidered in flowers, a leaden or an Indian-ink existence must surely have been a fearsome prospect. So was the world of Coketown, with its enforced 'wholesome monotony' [HT.II.i.111–12].

Since sameness or stasis is the beginning of the death of feeling, the Victorians love its opposite: violent contrasts. They loved even more those who could provide them with and promote in them excess of emotion and feeling.[15]Dickens's novels generate feeling by providing sudden and violent contrasts – between one mode of presentation and another, among other things, as we have seen. It is those violent contrasts that have been responsible for generating some of the richness of response in the modern reader as well. In his own life, Dickens 'facilitated feeling' by generating his own contrasts for himself: walking along the edge of Vesuvius, feeling the combined sensations of the chill mountain air and the hot, singeing lava. In his novels, he facilitated feeling by alternating comic and tragic scenes. He defended this world in which comic and tragic scenes followed each other in great rapidity 'in as regular alternation as the layers of red and white in a side of streaky well-cured bacon' [OT.xvii.118], by saying that

> such changes . . . are not so unnatural as they would seem at first sight. The transitions in real life from well-spread boards to death-beds, and from mourning weeds to holiday garments, are not a whit less startling; only, there, we are busy actors, instead of passive lookers-on, which makes a vast difference. The actors in the mimic life of the theatre, are blind to violent transitions and abrupt impulses of passion or feeling, which, presented before the eyes of mere spectators, are at once condemned as outrageous and preposterous [OT.xvii.118].

Those who are offended by these abrupt contrasts and alternations between the comic and tragic stand accused of being 'mere spectators' instead of participants in the drama. They are guilty of not 'feeling with' as much as they might be.

Those who are sensitive will appreciate the abrupt contrasts, the juxtaposing of the comic and the pathetic, the natural and the grotesque. The height of feeling is to be found in 'the one moment [when] joy and grief were mingled in the cup' [OT.li.401]. Nothing so deliciously combined the two as did the sight of a pantomimist dressed in clown's clothing, and bloated in belly from starvation [PP.iii.36]. Or the sight of ragged boys in *Oliver Twist* amusing themselves by jumping backwards and forwards over the coffin of a woman who has recently starved to death [OT.v.38]; nothing is so funny as the Misses Mould frolicking in father's funeral parlour [MC.xxv.403].

Still, the exact nature or content of the 'feeling' engendered in this way is difficult to specify. Exposure to rapidly alternating comic and tragic scenes or extreme mixes of comedy and the pathetic will make us 'feel' – much as plunging into alternating hot and cold baths will make us 'feel'. But feel what – other than the fact that we are feeling something? It may be that Dickens's world engenders in the reader something like what John Crowe Ransom talks about, a kind of revelling in our own feelings, however contentless they may be, because and simply because they are *our* feelings, and proof that we are not entirely numb.[16] It may also be true that violent contrasts do exactly what Dickens's peripheral world does, reminding us of the largeness of the world and the simultaneity of disparate and disjunctive events. We see young boys dancing back and forth over a new grave, and they remind us that while we grieve, others play, and that while we are playing, others grieve.

A close analysis of the part repetition plays in the generating of responses in readers of Dickens's novels, then, carries us a long way from the simple repeated phrase or gesture, that creates laughter: carries us over terrain where repetition implies the mechanical, the 'frozen up' and the static; over terrain where repetition suggests the possibility of human beings being incapable of change; over terrain where contrasts become violent enough to facilitate feeling in those whom mechanical repetition has made actually or potentially insensate.

The world was changing, transforming before Dickens's eyes. In his lifetime, the coaches he described so often in his novels were becoming obsolete, so that even for him, being 'Dickensian' required a conscious act of retrieving what was already in the past. In his later years, at Gad's Hill, Dickens often hired special coaches and rented special livery in crimson for those who drove them, so that he might give his guests a taste of the 'Dickensian'. As

Alexander Welsh reports,[17] the London Underground had been operating a full eight years before Dickens's death. Dickens's novels, then, in every possible way, provide a repertory of responses to a changing world. At times, we are dragged back into a colourful, nostalgic, pastoral past. What Steven Marcus says of George Eliot is equally true of Dickens: 'No longer able to believe what she once believed in in the past, she can at least reconstruct it imaginatively.'[18] Dickens reconstructed it in his descriptions and his rhetoric, and his readers still enjoy it. But Dickens was also aware of the pressures and threats of the present, and the necessity of living in that present. At some level of consciousness he knew that the best – the only way – to survive in that present and future, in which things are transforming before our eyes, with an old order disintegrated and a new order not yet fully formed, was to be prepared to change. To survive in the changing and transforming world in which railroads and horsepower were replacing horses, one needed to be constantly changing and transforming as the world changed. One needed to be always alert, and ready to shift one's responses to the world as necessity and change demanded.

So it is that in his use of repetition in the novels Dickens shows us not only how reassuring and funny repetitious behaviour can be, but how counter-productive as well. And just to make sure that the reader does not respond repetitiously to the world of his novels, comfortably smiling at his humour, or dissolving into self-indulgent tears at his pathos, Dickens constantly shifts his modes of presentation, thus ensuring his reader will do as he reads exactly what he must do to survive: be ever-vigilant, and prepared to shift his responses to the protean world engendered by Dickens's protean style, changing as it changes. 'Dickens created himself,' says Pearl Chester Solomon,[19] and he helps readers create themselves, too, giving them practice in dealing with and learning skills that are absolutely essential for survival: sorting out from the miscellany of events and details in life the crucial ones; patterning those crucial events and details to make meaning out of them; shifting responses to the world as events require; getting used to living in a world of contrasts; learning to be comfortable in a world in which a great many things require – urgently – to be changed, but in which, quite as much, the sheer complexity of the world thwarts our desire to change them.

7 One Reader Reading: the Reader in *The Old Curiosity Shop*

More than any other novel Dickens wrote, this one has tended to be rewritten in critical mythology and has become grossly oversimplified in the process.[1]

It is in the nature of the case that because a Dickens novel is so long and so full of detail and so full of different modes of presentation, readers can actualise that text in a number of very different ways, inevitably reducing its potential complexities and multiplicities of meaning. Nearly all critics of *The Old Curiosity Shop* begin with a perception of some radical disharmony in the novel. J. Hillis Miller notes the 'ironic identification of rural escape and death'.[2] Dickens talks in his rhetoric in the novel about the desirability and restfulness of the country, but what Nell and Trent find there is death. James Kincaid notes that 'for all the travelling and frantic rushing about that goes on, no one really moves anywhere or finally escapes from the pursuers'.[3] Steven Marcus notes that although Nell 'has moved through space she has travelled nowhere',[4] and suggests that the idyllic vision of *Oliver Twist* and *Nicholas Nickleby* begins to seem remote in *The Old Curiosity Shop*, and to become ambiguous and sentimental. Geoffrey Tillotson finds perhaps the most simple way of making any of the contradictions in a Dickens novel disappear: 'Dickens's amalgam of widely separate things has been made harmonious by their having issued from a mind that for each novel limited itself to one inexhaustible range of details – things of one complex colour – different as different continents differ for a geographer.'[5] What cannot be made consistent by reference to a theme can be made consistent simply by virtue of the fact that it is all in one novel, coming from one mind.

There would seem to be two tactics to adopt in the face of the fact that, as Marcus says, in *The Old Curiosity Shop,* 'at every turn, Dickens seemed entangled in contradictions'.[6] The first is simply to note the contradictions, pronounce them 'flaws' in Dickens's art, and move on. The second is to try to 'resolve' what is only 'apparently' a contradiction. Both Marcus and Kincaid end by doing the latter. 'The raging contraries of Quilp's sadism and masochism are the counterparts of the contradictory, sentimental emotions with which Dickens invested Nell,' says Marcus,[7] who goes on to explain the excessive sentiment as the consequence of Dickens's painful memories of the death of his sister-in-law Mary Hogarth at seventeen. Kincaid relies on a formal, aesthetic and psychological explanation for the apparent contradictions: 'Quilp allows our impulse to wring necks an outlet in laughter, so that the counter-impulse to protect and love the small and helpless might be expressed more fully. He is a very functional enemy of sentimentality.'[8]

Both of these are very sound, plausible and satisfying interpretations. However, both are also interpretations that can result only after – at the end of – the reading experience. What they leave out of account is the meaning that is generated *during* the reader's journey through the novel; the journey the reader takes while Nell and Trent are on their own journey through the novel. During the reading of *The Old Curiosity Shop*, the reader is not, I think, involved primarily or only in an attempt to resolve contradictions in Dickens's attitude towards the city or the country. It is perfectly true that, as Marcus says, there is a 'cleavage' in the novel, with the 'resulting image . . . of a radically divided sensibility, or two unrelated minds within one, each going its own autonomous way'.[9] But we do not read novels to be confirmed in our knowledge that the writer who wrote them has a 'radically divided sensibility'. There must be some other pleasure to be found in the novel that makes the reading experience worthwhile. What is the reader doing and enjoying, then, as he reads the novel?

I am pretty certain that what he is doing is not spending a great deal of time looking for clues to solve the 'mystery' at the heart of Dickens's plot, at least not in any conventional sense. There is, in the first place, much less mystery in this novel than there is in most of the other Dickens novels. Furthermore, the foreshadowing is so heavy-handed here that any reader with any alertness is destined to solve the mystery by the end of the first chapter of the novel. 'What if I had lost thee, Nell!' cries her grandfather [OCS.i.5]. The *if* here gives a clue to the mystery. 'His affection for the child might not be inconsistent with villainy of the worst kind,' says the narrator of Grandfather Trent [OCS.i.12], and that clue, too, is clear enough to catch the attention of any reader, in spite of the conditional. Nell seems 'rather to . . . lead and take care of [grandfather] than [he] to be protecting her' [OCS.i.5]. When Nell is momentarily lost, Kit Nubbles reassures Grandfather Trent, '*I'd* have found her, master, I'd have found her. I'd bet that I'd find her if she was above ground' [OCS.i.9], and the curiosity shop itself is 'dark and silent as the grave' [OCS.i.11]. On the very first page, Master Humphrey refers to the 'constant pacing to and fro, that never-ending restlessness, that incessant tread of feet wearing the rough stones smooth and glossy' [OCS.i.1].

So before the novel barely gets rolling, we know the whole story: there will be much wandering, Nell will lead Grandfather Trent, Grandfather will be responsible for some 'villainy' towards Nell, Nell will be lost, and she will be lost to the grave.

That the mystery isn't what interested Dickens most is evident in the terrible opacity of the prose that presumes to carry that mystery forward:

> Frederick Trent threw himself into a chair, and burying his head in his hands, endeavoured to fathom the motives which had led Quilp to insinuate himself into Richard Swiveller's confidence; – for that the disclosure was of his seeking, and had not been spontaneously revealed by Dick, was sufficiently plain from Quilp's seeking his company and enticing him away.
>
> The dwarf had twice encountered him when he was endeavouring to obtain intelligence of the fugitives. This, perhaps, as he had not shown any previous anxiety about them, was enough to awaken suspicion in the breast of a creature so jealous and distrustful by nature, setting aside any additional impulse to curiosity that he might have derived from Dick's incautious manner. But knowing the scheme they had planned, why should he offer to assist it? This was a question more difficult of solution; but as knaves generally overreach themselves by imputing their own designs to others, the idea immediately presented itself that some circumstances of irritation between Quilp and the old man, arising out of their secret transactions and not unconnected perhaps with his sudden disappearance, now rendered the former desirous of revenging himself upon him by seeking to entrap the

sole object of his love and anxiety into a connexion of which he
knew he had a dread and hatred [OCS.xxiii.173–4].

'Endeavouring to obtain intelligence' is hardly as clear as a simple
'trying to find out'. The confusions generated by the qualifiers and
litotes ('not unconnected perhaps'), among other things, guarantee
a crepuscularity of style and substance. There are several possible
explanations for this fact. Perhaps, since it is still relatively early in
Dickens's career, he had still a bit to learn about clarity. But this
hardly seems likely, given the vividness of which Dickens is capable
at other places in this novel, and in earlier pieces and novels as well.
Perhaps we might speculate that Dickens was trying somehow to
increase the general store of mystery in his novel by reproducing
some of that confusion and mystery in his narration as well as in his
descriptions. This explanation would be consistent with what
Roland Barthes calls the 'postulate of homology', which is that 'the
structure of the sentence, the object of linguistics, is found again,
homologically, in the structure of works'.[10] Perhaps the crowded,
confusing, dark and cluttered atmosphere of the curiosity shop is,
then, being reproduced in this cluttered and confusing prose.
Perhaps Dickens thought he was increasing the store of his mystery
by revealing his mystery only slowly and somewhat circum-
loquaciously. This kind of tactic is evident in Dickens's explanations
of Monks's relation to Oliver, or in the confusing account of the
confusing circumstances through which Jonas Chuzzlewit comes to
believe that he has poisoned his father when in fact he has not.
Perhaps this is just plain bad prose.

But the most logical explanation would seem to be that Dickens
was simply not that interested in his plot mystery, and consequently,
neither is the reader. If Dickens's mystery is easily solved in the first
few pages, and if his prose in conveying that mystery is confusing
and opaque, and if his theme is contradictory (the country is where
we want to be, but in the country all is stillness and death), why,
then, do we keep reading the novel? What is there to entertain and
satisfy and hold the attention of the reader? Some critics have
suggested that the novel appears to be more than anything else an
exploration and analysis of the phenomenon of death. What does it
feel like to be dead, to die, to be the one left behind when someone
else dies, to watch the death of a beautiful young girl. Surely the
novel spends a great deal of time speculating on these things – no
doubt because Dickens was still working through his feelings about

the death of Mary Hogarth – but I doubt that readers keep reading the novel because it is about death any more than they read it because it is a satisfying mystery story.

In reader-response criticism, it is the reading experience, its configurations and contours, that constitutes the meaning of the text. This does not mean that those themes – such as the exploration of death, or the analysis of city versus country life and exploration of the efficacy of each – are not present or plausible interpretations of *The Old Curiosity Shop*. However, to use, say, Stanley Fish's method of analysis, which is in his words 'an analysis of the developing responses of the reader to the words as they succeed one another on the page',[11] is to discover a different meaning in and to the text. As the reader of *The Old Curiosity Shop* moves from page to page in the novel, what he is destined to discover, I think, is that Dickens's ostensible theme is not interesting Dickens much at all. Rather, Dickens's attention keeps being drawn to the peripheral characters he is creating, and, as a result, the reader finds himself being drawn away from the central plot and actions as well. The experience of reading *The Old Curiosity Shop* becomes an experience in which we are constantly being pulled *away* from the ostensible centre of the novel, momentarily tugged back to that ostensible centre, and then pulled one more time away to that peripheral world. It is almost as if the novel we read and appreciate and respond to is the novel Dickens didn't or couldn't allow himself to write. It is the novel straining to be born; the novel Dickens wants to write but can't that attracts and holds our attention. One might say that what I have earlier called the peripheral world has managed to command the centre of our attention; has become the subject of the novel as, to some extent, it also does in *Little Dorrit*.

The first address to the reader from the narrator of *The Old Curiosity Shop* after the fading away of Master Humphrey concerns the sado-masochistic relationship of Quilp to the tumbling boy who serves him. The narrator says:

And here it may be remarked, that between this boy and the dwarf there existed a strange kind of mutual liking. How born or bred, or how nourished upon blows and threats on one side, and retorts and defiances on the other, is not to the purpose [OCS.v.42].

What is 'the purpose'? Presumably, that analysis of death and dying. But the meaning the text has for its readers here and at a hundred other points as well is quite different. What the reader must feel is that the narrator has set up an intriguing prospect, introduced an interesting subject, only to pull us back from it. It is the tease and promise of those worlds of speculation, and not the exploration of Death and Little Nell, I think, that keep readers reading *The Old Curiosity Shop*, and provide the most accurate description of the structure of the book. The reader plods along with Nell and her grandfather, through city streets and country pathways, but we would much prefer to wander off into that peripheral world of waxworks figures, circus performers, Punch and Judy shows, gamblers and tricksters, dwarfs and giants, Quilps and tumbling boys, rather than follow Nell and Dickens's 'theme'. In *Dombey and Son*, the issue of passion is fairly systematically explored almost, as it were, 'by the way', while pride is explored as the central concern of the novel. But in *The Old Curiosity Shop*, a whole host of interesting issues are raised, and then dropped, leaving the reader feeling that he has been introduced to a most interesting subject, only to be pulled away again. Sometimes the tease and promise is of an analysis of the strange sexual attractiveness of the sadistic dwarf. What do so many women find attractive about him? What does that say about women? About passion? Sometimes, the promise is of an analysis of gambling. Sometimes, Dickens promises an analysis of rumour; sometimes, of honesty and its rewards and dangers. Codlin tries to outdo Short, and Short, Codlin. Nell can't even trust her grandfather. Foxey Brass's motto, 'Always suspect everybody' [OCS.lxvi.499], might be taken to be the theme of the novel. The Brasses try to trick Kit Nubbles, and are tricked in return. Everyone gossips, and rumour might be seen to be the major villain in the novel: Kit Nubbles is the victim of rumour; it is rumour (of their presumed wealth) that sets Nell and Grandfather on their fateful journey. But none of these intriguing prospects is ever actualised in and by the text, so that what *is* actualised is the experience of being introduced to a subject, and then drawn away from it.

In his book *Beginnings*, Edward Said suggests that 'the text' of an author really consists of the entire corpus of that author's works, and that readers make sense of each work in the context that includes all of his works.[12] The reader of *The Old Curiosity Shop* who knows other Dickens novels, then, will make sense of that novel by noting that in one sense, the peripheral world of suffering paupers and wandering people that we expect to find on the fringes of Dickens's world has in

The Old Curiosity Shop moved to the centre of the plot. But this hardly means that there is no peripheral world in the novel. Instead, Dickens has created two other peripheral realms that surround the 'central' peripheral world created by Nell and the wanderings she goes through with her grandfather. One peripheral world is that which I have already touched upon: the world of speculation about sado-masochism, about gossip and rumour; about the whole question raised also in Melville's *The Confidence-Man*: whom should we trust. The second peripheral world is a more exaggerated world of suffering than that at the centre of the novel. The grotesques, like the old pawnbroker with claws who cries "O goroo goroo!" at David Copperfield, have become concentrated in the person of all those wax figures in Mrs Jarley's waxworks:

> Jasper Packlemerton of atrocious memory, who courted and married fourteen wives, and destroyed them all, by tickling the soles of their feet when they were sleeping in the consciousness of innocence and virtue . . . . The old lady who died of dancing at a hundred and thirty-two, the wild boy of the woods, the woman who poisoned fourteen families with pickled walnuts . . . [OCS.xxviii.214].

They are both funny and horrible. For the unfunny world of misery on the peripheries, we have reports, such as that of the narrator who talks of a bridge, where 'some, of a very different class, pause with heavier loads than they, remembering to have heard or read in some old time that drowning was not a hard death, but of all means of suicide the easiest and best' [OCS.i.2]. Or we have the house at which Nell stops for bread, and is greeted at the door by a man who says, 'Do you see that? . . . That's a dead child. I and five hundred other men were thrown out of work, three months ago. That is my third dead child, and last' [OCS.xlv.337].

What kind of rhetorical control and social commentary do we find in *The Old Curiosity Shop* to contain these miseries that exist in, as it were, the world beyond the Dickens world? We have what I have already described. To the problem of the five hundred out-of-work men and their starving babies whose dead bodies are heaped in the corners of hovels, Dickens provides his usual artificed and artificial conclusion: Nell's response is to shriek, pass out senseless on the ground – where, luckily she falls just at the feet of the schoolmaster who has already demonstrated his kindliness and humanity. Nell, we know, will be saved, and it will be accident or Fate that has saved her. Such accidents of Fate hardly seem to be consistent with Dickens's rhetorical protestations that miseries of the sort embodied in the scene with the impoverished worker can be alleviated if only 'those that rule the destinies of men' would become more sensitive to the needs of the poor. As is usual in Dickens's novels, there is rhetorical admonition in and of the most urgent terms, but it rarely coincides with the action of the plot:

> Oh! if those that rule the destinies of nations would but remember this – if they would but think how hard it is for the very poor to have engendered in their hearts, that love of home from which all domestic virtues spring, when they live in dense and squalid masses where social decency is lost, or rather never found, – if they would but turn aside from the wide thoroughfares and great houses, and strive to improve the wretched dwellings in bye-ways where only Poverty may walk, – many low roofs would point more truly to the sky, than the loftiest steeple that now rears proudly up from the midst of guilt, and crime, and horrible disease, to mock them by its contrast. . . . In love of home, the love of country has its rise; and who are the truer patriots or the better in time of need – those who venerate the land, owning its wood and stream, and earth, and all they produce? or those who love their country, boasting not a foot of ground in all its wide domain! [OCS.xxxviii.282]

This should sound very familiar; it is identical to the kind of rhetorical protestations one finds in *Bleak House*, in *Little Dorrit* and in *Oliver Twist*. Home is a sanctuary, a haven, and a solution to the problems of the world. But as we have seen in Chapter V, Dickens's rhetoric here is inconsistent with what happens in his plots. Whose hearth is hallowed in *The Old Curiosity Shop*? Quilp's? The Brass's? For every Nubbles household, there is a Quilp household; for every Garland cottage, an Old Curiosity Shop. The Brass siblings are not impoverished, and yet their house is very much spiritually impoverished.

Even around the issue of death, Dickens's ostensible subject, we find a narrator whose pronouncements are not to be trusted. In *The Old Curiosity Shop*, death is both the subject of serious rhetoric, and the occasion for jokes:

> The clergyman's horse . . . was cropping the grass; at once deriving orthodox consolation from the dead parishioners, and enforcing last Sunday's text that this was what all flesh came to [OCS.xxvi.122].

More than once death becomes the occasion for jokes the narrator wants to tell. We could say, as I have said of Dombey and Edith's wedding in *Dombey and Son*, that Dickens's subject is not death (or weddings), but an exploration of all the attitudes it is possible to take towards death (or weddings).

Dickens's tendency to lapse into blank verse in *The Old Curiosity Shop* (and elsewhere, as a matter of fact), has been mentioned often. Just at the point at which the references to death begin in *The Old Curiosity Shop*, the blank verse begins as well:

> The child . . . had but feebly described the sadness and sorrow of her thoughts, or the heaviness of the cloud which overhung her home, and cast dark shadows on its hearth [OCS.ix.68].

The reader presumes that he is to take Little Nell's plight seriously. But the rhythm of the prose in which her plight is conveyed to us is so dangerously and distressingly similar to that we have read only a page earlier, in Dick Swiveller's poem to Sophy Wackles:

> I would that I had been my own mistress too
> . . . before I had ever entertained a thought of you.
> Miss Wackles, I believed you true, and I
> was blest in so believing,
> but now I mourn that e'er I knew,
> a girl so fair yet so deceiving [OCS.viii.67].

Whatever syntactical or rhetorical pattern Dickens or his narrator proffer seriously one instant, he satirises in the person and prose of Dick Swiveller the next, and knowledge of that fact is part of the experience of reading *The Old Curiosity Shop*, and part of its meaning as well. Dick Swiveller was Dickens's favourite character in the novel, and perhaps this is so because in the person of Dick Swiveller Dickens could make fun of his own propensities to sentimental rhetoric in the rest of the novel. As Nell and her grandfather set out on their long journey that will end in death, Dickens's narrator announces: 'Forth from the city, while it yet slumbered, went the

two poor adventurers, wandering they knew not whither'
[OCS.xii.96]. The halting, comma-ridden sentence may slow down
the reading of the sentence, making it more sombre – making it even
somewhat reverent, since the diction is more than vaguely biblical.
The reader is sure, then, that he is to take this sentiment seriously.
But Dick Swiveller is prone to announce such things as that he was
'wafted here upon the pinions of concord; that I came to remove,
with the rake of friendship, the seeds of mutual wiolence and heart-
burning, and to sow in their place, the germs of social harmony'
[OCS.xiii.103].

James Kincaid suggests that '*The Old Curiosity Shop*, for all its
hatred of Little Bethel, uses evangelical rhetoric and clearly expects
something like a religious conversion to Nellyism. In this expectation, then, the novel is clearly antagonistic, implying that a failure
of response is not an aesthetic but a spiritual failure.'[13] I think he is
almost right, since while it is true that Dickens does resort to that
evangelical rhetoric and expect a 'religious conversion to Nellyism',
at the same time his style systematically and regularly undercuts
and satirises his own evangelical rhetoric, usually in the person
of Dick Swiveller, though sometimes even in the rhetoric of
Mr Garland and Witherden the Notary. Thus the novel is not quite
so 'antagonistic' as Kincaid suggests, though it is surely rich in
possibilities for response, as the reader is encouraged first to respond
negatively to the evangelical rhetoric (when he meets Dickens's
antagonistic portrayal of the real Little Bethel and Mrs Nubbles's
involvement in it), then positively (when he meets Dickens's
own evangelical rhetoric), and finally, negatively again (when
he encounters Dickens's own satirical attacks on that same
rhetoric).

Stanley Fish's recommendation to critics is that they stop asking
'what does this sentence mean?' or 'what is it about?' or 'what
is it saying?' in favour of the question 'what does this sentence
do?' or 'what is this passage doing?'[14] I would suggest that the
latter are the only possible questions to ask of Dickens's prose here
as well. What Dickens's prose is doing, here, as everywhere else,
is trying out attitudes, and Dickens's subject, then, is not
evangelical rhetoric like that of Little Bethel, but instead an
exploration of the possible attitudes one can adopt towards such
rhetoric – including laughter. And, to the extent that Dickens's
prose makes us encounter in rapid sequence one attitude and then
another, his subject itself becomes change: how to change attitudes

rapidly. His novel provides, in effect, practice in rapid changing of attitude.

Dickens also gives his readers practice in changing attitudes by providing them with a multitude of those prophetic *ifs* that I have talked about. Sometimes, Dickens's *ifs* are of the kind that evade and avoid recommending radical solutions to economic and social problems, as they do in the passage cited above, in which Nell encounters the impoverished labourer and the dead child in the corner. Sometimes, Dickens's *ifs* both evade and express, simultaneously, some 'inexpressible' desire: Mrs. Quilp muses, 'If I was to die tomorrow, Quilp could marry anybody he pleased. . . . The best looking woman here couldn't refuse him if I was dead, and she was free, and he chose to make love to her' [OCS.iv.32]. This kind of evasion that avoids explicit acknowledgement of sexual power reminds me of the kind of evasion Steven Marcus says George Eliot employs in 'The Sad Fortunes of the Revd Amos Barton', and it manages both to evade and to convey both the reason for the mysterious happiness of Mrs Barton (her husband's fantastic passion and potency), and for her death (too many pregnancies, the result of her husband's fantastic passion and potency).[15] (Quilp, of course, is also sexually potent. There's no other explanation for why Mrs Quilp endures him and thinks without doubt that any other woman would want him. Quilp's usual threat of 'I'll bite you!' is said by critics to be harmless because it is so much the threat of a small child. But it is quite as likely to be a sexual threat and/or promise. ' "Oh you nice creature!" were the words with which [Quilp] broke the silence; smacking his lips as if this were no figure of speech, and she were actually a sweetmeat. "Oh you precious darling! oh you delicious charmer!" ' he says [OCS.iv.35], and I leave my reader to go to the text to discover exactly where Quilp's head is as he pronounces these words [OCS.iv.36].)

So the *if* evades social/political statement; it evades explicit sexual reference; it introduces the notion of Fate into the otherwise Christian world and Christian rationales of *The Old Curiosity Shop*:

> The old man sat poring over the cards, dealing them as they had been dealt before, and turning up the different hands to see what each man would have held if they had still been playing. . . . If I could have gone on a little longer [OCS.xxx.225–6].

The *if* introduces cynical notes that Dickens cannot tolerate or face or introduce straightforwardly. Early in the novel, for instance, Nell muses of her grandfather that:

> If he were to die – if sudden illness had happened to him, and he were never to come home again, alive, – if, one night, he should come home, and kiss and bless her as usual, and after she had gone to bed and had fallen asleep and was perhaps dreaming pleasantly, and smiling in her sleep, he should kill himself and his blood come creeping, creeping, on the ground to her bed-room door! . . . [OCS.ix.69–70]

Nell's wish or thought is never completed, and the incompleted sentence and the *if* express not only the child's secret wish, but, I think, both Dickens's and his readers' as well. If we could all get out of that curiosity shop and get rid of Grandfather and the wanderings and the exploration of death, we could all get back to the world of Quilp and Wackles. When Nell's musings trail off, the narrator adds, 'These thoughts were too terrible to dwell upon' [OCS.ix.70]. Because Dickens cannot let this cup pass away; because Dickens needed to work out his feelings about death and, specifically, the death of Mary Hogarth, 'so young, so beautiful, so good' [OCS.lxxii.542], the reader, Nell, and Dickens are all stuck with the story of youthful death. Kincaid says that the 'quietness' Dickens worked for and achieved in the atmosphere of this novel 'there is an underlying bitterness and a dominant motif of retribution which makes this quietness much more sinister and dark than soft and sad.'[16] I detect a 'quietness' in this novel, but it seems to be a quietness that comes because we are all trapped in an immobility generated by the equal force of two opposing impulses: the one towards the central subject of death, and the other resolutely away from that subject. All the while we are exploring peace, serenity and, ultimately, death, in the country, Dickens keeps straining to offer us instead all of the interest and energy and life of the city slickers, hustlers and hucksters, and the reading experience we have is that of being lured off into that more lively world, and then being reluctantly dragged back to the central world of serenity and death. *The Old Curiosity Shop* that we read and re-read is not the one Dickens wrote, but the one he couldn't quite write: the novel he strains towards, promises and sometimes delivers – the world of life and energy and comedy that goes on in spite of the death at the centre.

Notes

PREFACE

1. M. A. K. Halliday, 'Linguistic Function and Literary Style', in Seymour Chatman (ed.) *Literary Style* (London: Oxford, 1971) p. 330.
2. Leo Spitzer, 'Pseudoobjektive Motivierung bei Charles-Louis Philippe', in *Stilstudien* (Munich: 1961) p. 166.
3. Roman Jakobson, 'Linguistics and Poetics', in Thomas Sebeok (ed.) *Style in Language* (Cambridge, Mass.: M.I.T. Press, 1960) p. 358.
4. Jonathan Culler, *Structuralist Poetics* (Ithaca, N.Y.: Cornell University Press, 1975) p. 66.
5. Ibid., p. 65.
6. Berel Lang, 'Style as Instrument, Style as Person', *Critical Inquiry*, IV:4 (Summer 1978) p. 716.
7. Ibid.
8. Roman Jakobson, p. 377.
9. Ross Chambers, 'Commentary in Literary Texts', *Critical Inquiry*, V:2 (Winter 1978) p. 323.
10. Seymour Chatman, *Story and Discourse* (Ithaca, N.Y.: Cornell University Press, 1978).
11. Thomas S. Kuhn, *The Essential Tension* (Chicago and London: University of Chicago Press, 1977) p. xvii.
12. G. K. Chesterton, *Charles Dickens* (New York: The Press of the Readers Club, 1942) p. 60; rpt of *Charles Dickens: A Critical Study* (New York: Dodd Mead & Co., 1906).
13. Albert Guerard, *The Triumph of the Novel* (London: Oxford University Press, 1976).
14. Barbara Hardy, *The Moral Art of Charles Dickens* (London: Athlone Press, 1970).
15. Albert Guerard, p. 143.
16. Alexander Welsh, *The City in Dickens* (Oxford: Clarendon Press, 1971) p. 10.
17. Frank Kermode, *The Classic: Literary Images of Permanence and Change* (New York: Viking Press, 1975) p. 118.
18. Albert Guerard, p. 4.
19. Wolfgang Iser, 'Indeterminacy and the Reader's Response in Prose Fiction', in J. Hillis Miller (ed.) *Aspects of Narrative* (New York: Columbia University Press, 1971) p. 40.
20. Stanley E. Fish, 'How to Do Things with Austin and Searle: Speech Act Theory and Literary Criticism', in Richard A. Macksey and Henry Sussman (eds) *Responsibilities of the Critic, Modern Language Notes*, 91 (1976) p. 996.

21. René Girard, 'Critical Reflections on Literary Studies', in Richard Macksey (ed.) *Velocities of Change: Critical Essays from Modern Language Notes* (Baltimore and London: Johns Hopkins University Press, 1974) p. 78.

22. Susan R. Horton, *Interpreting Interpreting: Interpreting Dickens's Dombey* (Baltimore and London: Johns Hopkins University Press, 1979).

1 INTRODUCTION

1. I. A. Richards, *Principles of Literary Criticism* (New York: Harcourt, Brace & World, 1925) pp. 22–3.

2. G. K. Chesterton, *Charles Dickens* (New York: Press of the Readers Club, 1942) p. 257; rpt of *Charles Dickens: A Critical Study* (New York: Dodd Mead & Co., 1906).

3. Mario Praz, 'Charles Dickens', in *The Hero in Eclipse in Victorian Fiction*, tr. Angus Davidson (London: Oxford University Press, 1956) p. 172.

4. E. M. Forster, *Aspects of the Novel* (New York: Harcourt, Brace & World, 1927) p. 72.

2 INTENTION, TEXT AND RESPONSE

1. Wolfgang Iser, 'Indeterminacy and the Reader's Response in Prose Fiction', in J. Hillis Miller (ed.), *Aspects of Narrative* (New York: Columbia University Press, 1971) pp. 43–5.

2. Ibid., p. 8.

3. John Butt and Kathleen Tillotson, *Dickens at Work* (London: Methuen, 1957) p. 16.

4. George Ford, *Dickens and his Readers* (Princeton: Princeton University Press, 1955) p. 12.

5. Quoted by Ford, p. 31.

6. Walter Bagehot, 'Charles Dickens', in *National Review* VII (October 1858) p. 80.

7. Quoted by Edgar Johnson in *Charles Dickens: His Tragedy and Triumph* (New York: Simon & Schuster, 1952) II, 1057.

8. Charles Dickens, *Letters*, ed. Walter Dexter (London: Nonesuch, 1938), II, 695.

9. Charles Dickens, quoted by Stephen Wall in *Charles Dickens* (Baltimore: Penguin Books, 1970) p. 63.

10. In a letter to the Hon. Mrs R. Watson, 7 December 1857.

11. From a speech Dickens gave on 26 February 1844 to the Mechanics Institute, p. 57 in K. J. Fielding's edition of the *Speeches*. For a more complete cataloguing of Dickens's social and political ambivalences (his attraction to and repulsion from will and assertiveness, and his fascination with and fear of the railroad and all the trappings of the new industrial order, for instance, see Steven Marcus, *Dickens: From Pickwick to Dombey* (London: Chatto & Windus, 1965) and for the same kind of catalogue of some of Dickens's moral ambivalences (a leaning toward both the *lex talionis* morality and Christian

love and forgiveness) see Harvey Peter Sucksmith, *The Narrative Art of Charles Dickens* (London: Oxford University Press, 1970).

12. Alexander Welsh, *The City in Dickens* (Oxford: Clarendon Press, 1971) pp. 64–5.

13. Pearl Chester Solomon, *Dickens and Melville in Their Time* (New York: Columbia University Press, 1975) p. 23.

14. Northrop Frye has suggested that our seeing what a literary work means is always a response 'not simply to *the* whole *of* it, but to *a* whole *in* it'; we have a vision of meaning,' he says, 'whenever any simultaneous apprehension is possible.' (*Anatomy of Criticism*, Princeton: Princeton University Press, 1957) p. 78. I have taken this to mean that meaning accrues to a work of literature not only as a result of the reader's apprehension of the symbolic and imagic patterns there are in the work, or out of the reader's recognition of the plot and the interactions of its characters and the resolution of that plot, but also out of the reader's perception of the interaction of and relation of one stylistic trait or one mode of presentation and another; out of the way that rhetoric either enforces or denies image, for instance. This approach, it seems to me, is capable of uncovering rich veins of meaning not only in Dickens's novels, but in a great many other of those novels that would fall under Henry James's terribly over-used category of the 'loose and baggy monster', or novels comprised of more than one tone, attitude, narrative voice, or mode of presentation. Surely Theodore Dreiser's novels, for instance, as well as Herman Melville's works, are prime candidates for this kind of analysis?

3 SEQUENCE AND CONSEQUENCE

1. J. Hillis Miller, 'Three Problems of Fictional Form: First-Person Narration in *David Copperfield* and *Huckleberry Finn*', in Roy Harvey Pearce (ed.) *Experience in the Novel* (New York: Columbia University Press, 1968) p. 23.

2. Steven Marcus, *Dickens: from Pickwick to Dombey* (London: Chatto & Windus, 1965) p. 171.

3. Seymour Chatman, *Story and Discourse* (Ithaca, N.Y.: Cornell University Press, 1978) p. 23.

4. Steven Marcus, 'Human Nature, Social Orders, and 19th Century Systems of Explanation: Starting In with George Eliot', *Salmagundi*, No. 28 (Winter 1975) p. 24.

5. This is the major thesis of Robert Garis's book *The Dickens Theatre* (London: Oxford University Press, 1965).

6. Edgar Johnson, *Charles Dickens: His Tragedy and Triumph* (New York: Simon & Schuster, 1952) II, 752–3.

7. Ibid., p. 293.

8. Ibid.

9. R. P. Blackmur, 'The Craft of Herman Melville: A Putative Statement', in *The Expense of Greatness* (Gloucester, Mass.: Peter Smith, 1958) p. 87. This essay is also collected in *The Lion and the Honeycomb: Essays in Solicitude and Critique* (New York: Harcourt, Brace & World, 1955).

10. Ibid.

11. Christopher Hibbert, *The Making of Charles Dickens* (New York: Harper & Row, 1967).
12. Walter Dexter, *Letters of Charles Dickens* (London: Nonesuch, 1938) I, 185.
13. Ibid.
14. Charles Dickens, 'State of the Soldiers', *The Uncommercial Traveller*, p. 77.

4 THE READER AT WORK

I The Rhetorics of Image and Idea

1. Ross Chambers, 'Commentary in Literary Texts', *Critical Inquiry*, V:2 (Winter 1978) p. 335.
2. Kenneth Burke, *A Rhetoric of Motives* (Berkeley: University of California Press, 1969) p. 89.
3. See Emile Benveniste, *Problèmes de Linguistique générale*, 2 vols (Paris, 1966, 1974) especially 'L'Homme dans la langue'.
4. Ross Chambers, p. 323.
5. See Harvey Peter Sucksmith, *The Narrative Art of Charles Dickens* (Oxford: Clarendon Press, 1970) p. 68. Brackets in this passage indicate words Dickens cancelled at proof stage; words in capital letters indicate words added at proof stage.
6. See Wayne Booth, *The Rhetoric of Fiction* (Chicago: University of Chicago Press, 1961) p. 182, as well as all of his Chapter 7, 'The Uses of Reliable Commentary'.
7. Ross Chambers, p. 326.
8. John Crowe Ransom, *The World's Body* (Baton Rouge: Louisiana State University Press, 1968) p. 131.
9. Steven Marcus, 'Human Nature, Social Orders, and 19th Century Systems of Explanation: Starting In with George Eliot', *Salmagundi*, No. 28 (Winter 1975) p. 25.
10. Simon Lesser, *Fiction and the Unconscious* (Boston: Beacon Press, 1957) p. 175.
11. John Crowe Ransom, p. 115.
12. John Butt and Kathleen Tillotson's account of the note Dickens made for *Great Expectations* in his General Memo shows Dickens's moral intent was strong. The note reads, 'So goes abroad to Herbert (happily married to Clara Barley), and becomes his clerk. The one good thing he did in his prosperity, the only thing that endures and bears good fruit.' See *Dickens at Work* (London: Methuen, 1957) p. 31.
13. Geoffrey Tillotson, *A View of Victorian Literature* (London: Oxford University Press, 1978) pp. 124–5.
14. Simon Lesser, p. 154.
15. Ibid.
16. See Lesser, p. 248, as well as Norman N. Holland, *The Dynamics of Literary Response* (New York: Oxford University Press, 1968) pp. 68–9.
17. See my discussion of repetition as productive of both comfort and threat in Chapter VI, part 3.
18. John Butt and Kathleen Tillotson, *Dickens at Work*, p. 46.

19. Barbara Hardy, *The Moral Art of Charles Dickens* (London: Athlone Press, 1970) p. 13.

2 Rhetoric and Plot

1. F. R. and Q. D. Leavis, *Dickens the Novelist* (New York: Random House, 1970) p. 171.
2. Ibid.
3. Seymour Chatman, *Story and Discourse* (Ithaca, N.Y.: Cornell University Press, 1978) p. 44.
4. F. R. Leavis, *The Great Tradition* (New York: New York University Press, 1963) p. 228; rpt. first published, London, Chatto & Windus, 1950.
5. Quoted in Stephen Wall, *Charles Dickens* (New York: Penguin Books, 1970) p. 48.
6. Ibid., p. 138.
7. Ibid., pp. 124–5.
8. Wolfgang Iser, 'Indeterminacy and the Reader's Response in Prose Fiction', in J. Hillis Miller (ed.), *Aspects of Narrative* (New York: Columbia University Press, 1971) pp. 18–19.
9. This is John Crowe Ransom's formulation, in *The World's Body* (Baton Rouge: Louisiana State University Press, 1968) p. 282.
10. G. K. Chesterton, *Charles Dickens* (New York: Press of the Readers Club, 1942) pp. 27–28; rpt of *Charles Dickens: A Critical Study* (New York: Dodd Mead & Co., 1906).
11. John Forster, *Life of Charles Dickens*, ed. J. W. T. Ley (New York: Doubleday, Doran & Co., 1928) p. 638.
12. Charles Dickens, *Letters*, ed. Walter Dexter, II (London, 1938) p. 695.
13. See George Bernard Shaw's Introduction Epistolary to Arthur Bingham Walkley in *Man and Superman*, in *The Plays of George Bernard Shaw* (New York: New American Library, 1960) p. 255.
14. Theodore Dreiser, *Sister Carrie*, ed. Donald Pizer (New York: W. W. Norton & Co., 1970) p. 1.

3 The Reticent Rhetorician

1. Ross Chambers, 'Commentary in Literary Texts', *Critical Inquiry*, V:2 (Winter 1978) p. 327.
2. Robert Garis, *The Dickens Theatre* (Oxford: Clarendon Press, 1965) p. 174.
3. F. R. and Q. D. Leavis, *Dickens the Novelist* (New York: Random House, 1970) p. 120.
4. Ibid., pp. 120–2.
5. See the *Letters from Charles Dickens to Angela Burdett-Coutts, 1841–1865*, ed. Edgar Johnson (London, 1953) p. 165.
6. Gérard Genette, 'Vraisemblance et motivation', in *Figures* II (Paris, 1969) pp. 71–99.
7. Ross Chambers, p. 327.
8. See Harvey Peter Sucksmith, *The Narrative Art of Charles Dickens* (Oxford: Clarendon Press, 1970), and James R. Kincaid, *Dickens and the Rhetoric of Laughter* (Oxford: Clarendon Press, 1971) for an extensive treatment of this phenomenon.

9. See James Kincaid, p. 54. 'It is impossible', he says, 'to define the characteristics or moral positions of the narrator in this novel, for they are constantly shifting. It is true that, as in most Dickens novels, the narrative voice provides a counterpoint to the story and gives oblique directions to the reader. But here the directions are generally misleading. We expect those obtrusive narrative commentaries at least to provide accurate signposts to a comfortable position we can take, but here Dickens exploits this very expectation to attack smug confidence.'
10. See my Chapter VI for a more detailed analysis of this phenomenon.
11. Paul Goodman, *The Structure of Literature* (Chicago: University of Chicago Press, 1954) p. 256.
12. Ibid.

4 The Rhetoric of Seems

1. SB.vi.76.
2. MED.xxiii.270.
3. LD.I.xvii.205.
4. Wayne Booth, *The Rhetoric of Fiction* (Chicago: University of Chicago Press, 1961) p. 184.
5. In *David Copperfield*, for instance, as Steerforth walks along the shore, he muses that 'the sea roars as if it were hungry for us' (DC.xxi.311), and, as we know, the sea does turn out to be 'hungry' for Steerforth. After Eugene Wrayburn and Mortimer Lightwood stand by the shore waiting for Gaffer Hexam, Wrayburn says, 'I feel as if I had been half-drowned, and swallowing a gallon of it' (OMF.I.xiii.164), which is precisely what is to happen to him later in the novel.
6. Wayne Booth, *The Rhetoric of Fiction*, p. 184.
7. Ross Chambers, p. 335.

5 THE WORLD BEYOND THE DICKENS WORLD

1 Dickens's Peripheral Vision

1. W. H. Auden, 'Musée Des Beaux Arts'.
2. MC.xxix.462.
3. Nikolai Gogol, *Dead Souls*, tr. Andrew R. MacAndrew (New York: New American Library, 1961) p. 20.
4. Ibid., p. 165.
5. Ibid., p. 148.
6. See Maynard Mack's Introduction to *Joseph Andrews* (New York: Rinehart, 1948) p. xvi in which he remarks that 'even a rabbit, were it suddenly to materialise before us without complicity, could be a terrifying event. What makes us laugh is our secure consciousness of the magician and his hat.' Dickens's peripheral characters are often like rabbits appearing without the aid of either magician or hat, and disconcerting insofar as and whenever this is true.
7. Kenneth Burke, *A Rhetoric of Motives* (Berkeley: University of California Press, 1969) p. 115.

8. The progenitor of this practice is Jingle in *Pickwick Papers*, who recounts the story of the unfortunate woman who loses her head this way: 'Heads, heads— take care of your heads! . . . Terrible place—dangerous work—other day— five children—mother—tall lady, eating sandwiches—forgot the arch— crash—knock—children look round—mother's head off—sandwich in her hand—no mouth to put it in—head of a family off—shocking, shocking!' (PP.ii.11).
9. See James Kincaid, *Dickens and the Rhetoric of Laughter*, for an account of how Dickens makes us both laugh at such escapades and accounts, and im- mediately feel guilty for laughing.
10. F. R. and Q. D. Leavis, *Dickens the Novelist*, p. 272.
11. Sylvia Bank Manning, *Dickens as Satirist* (New Haven and London: Yale University Press, 1971) p. 168.
12. Quoted by George Ford in *Dickens and His Readers* (Princeton: Princeton University Press, 1955) p. 41.
13. Quoted by Steven Marcus in *Dickens: from Pickwick to Dombey* (London: Chatto & Windus, 1965) p. 61.
14. From a letter of Dickens's, quoted by Edgar Johnson in *The Heart of Charles Dickens* (Boston: Little Brown & Co., 1952) p. 370.
15. Steven Marcus, *Dickens: from Pickwick to Dombey*, p. 278.
16. John Forster, *Life*, p. 424.
17. Ibid., p. 641.

2 The Huddle

1. LD.I.xi.124.
2. OT.xxiii.165.
3. Leo Marx, *The Machine in the Garden* (London: Oxford University Press, 1964) pp. 19, 32.
4. Alexander Welsh, *The City in Dickens* (Oxford: Clarendon Press, 1971) p. 162.

3 The Double Vision

1. Wayne Booth, *The Rhetoric of Fiction* (Chicago: University of Chicago Press, 1961) p. 136.
2. Barbara Hardy, *The Moral Art of Charles Dickens* (London: Athlone Press, 1970) p. 11.
3. H. M. Daleski, *Dickens and the Art of Analogy* (New York: Shocken Books, 1970).
4. John Forster, *Life*, p. 650.
5. See John Butt and Kathleen Tillotson, *Dickens at Work* (London: Methuen & Co., 1957) pp. 33–4, for a more detailed account of these note pages and their probable function.
6. George Orwell, 'Charles Dickens', in *The Collected Essays, Journalism, and Letters of George Orwell*, eds. Sonia Orwell and Ian Angus (New York: Harcourt, Brace & World, 1968) I, 417.
7. E. M. Forster, *Aspects of the Novel* (New York: Harcourt, Brace & World, 1927.) p. 95.
8. Simon Lesser, *Fiction and the Unconscious* (Boston: Beacon Press, 1957) p. 185.

9. Yrjo Hirn, 'Art the Reliever', in *A Modern Book Of Aesthetics*, ed. Melvin M. Rader (New York: Holt, 1935) p. 110.
10. Norman N. Holland, *The Dynamics of Literary Response* (New York: Oxford University Press, 1968) pp. 164–5.
11. Geoffrey Hartman, *The Fate of Reading* (Chicago: University of Chicago Press, 1975) p. 209.
12. E. M. Forster, p. 96.
13. Kenneth Burke, p. 270.

4 *The Time Telscope and the Labyrinth of the Conditional*

1. H. A. Taine, *History of English Literature*, trans. H. Van Laun (New York: John Wurtele Lovell, 1873) p. 591.
2. William J. Harvey, *Character and the Novel* (Ithaca, N.Y.: Cornell University Press, 1965) p. 142.
3. See Forster's *Life*, p. 491.
4. Thomas Carlyle, 'The Present Time', in *Latter Day Pamphlets*, in the Centenary Edition of Carlyle's Works, ed. H. D. Traill, 30 vols (New York: 1896–1901); (rpt in 1 vol., New York: A.M.S. Press, 1969) p. 15.
5. Quoted by Leo Marx, *The Machine in the Garden*, p. 121.
6. Ibid., p. 157.
7. Joseph Wood Krutch, *Experience and Art* (New York: Smith & Haas, 1932) pp. 63–4.
8. Taylor Stoehr, *Dickens: The Dreamer's Stance* (Ithaca, N.Y.: Cornell University Press, 1965).

6 THE DYNAMICS OF DESCRIPTION

1 Description as Re-creation

1. Steven Marcus, *Dickens: from Pickwick to Dombey* (London: Chatto & Windus, 1965) pp. 63–4.
2. Robert Garis, *The Dickens Theatre* (London: Oxford University Press, 1965) p. 109.
3. I. A. Richards, *Principles of Literary Criticism* (New York: Harcourt, Brace & World, 1925) p. 240.
4. I. A. Richards, *Practical Criticism* (New York: Harcourt, Brace & World, 1929) p. 210.
5. William J. Harvey, *Character and the Novel* (Ithaca, N.Y.: Cornell University Press, 1965) p. 37.
6. Donald Fanger, *Dostoevsky and Romantic Realism* (Chicago: University of Chicago Press, 1967) p. viii.
7. William Faulkner, *Light in August* (New York: Random House, 1950) p. 4.
8. Rudolf Arnheim, *Visual Thinking* (Berkeley: University of Chicago Press, 1971) p. 37.
9. George Orwell, 'Charles Dickens', in *The Collected Essays*, ed. Sonia Orwell and Ian Angus (New York: Harcourt, Brace & World, 1968) p. 454.

2 Description as Defence

1. George Bernard Shaw, Introduction Epistolary to Arthur Bingham Walkley in *Man and Superman*, in *The Plays of George Bernard Shaw* (New York: New American Library, 1960) p. 256.

3 Descriptions and Repetitions

1. Norman N. Holland, *The Dynamics of Literary Response* (London: Oxford University Press, 1968) p. 146.
2. Henri Bergson, 'Laughter', in *Comedy*, ed. Wylie Sypher (New York: Doubleday Anchor Books, 1956) p. 97.
3. Jonathan Culler, *Structuralist Poetics* (Ithaca, N.Y.: Cornell University Press, 1975) p. 71.
4. Henri Bergson, 'Laughter', p. 100.
5. Simon O. Lesser, *Fiction and the Unconscious* (Boston: Beacon Press, 1957) pp. 6–7.
6. Otto Fenichel, *The Psychoanalytic Theory of Neurosis* (New York: W. W. Norton & Co., 1945) p. 373.
7. Bernard Schilling, in *The Comic Spirit: Boccaccio to Thomas Mann* (Detroit: Wayne State University Press, 1965) p. 108, recognises this fact too, when he says that Micawber 'finds the cure and relief of suffering in its expression'.
8. Henri Bergson, 'Laughter', pp. 72–3.
9. Bruce F. Kawin, *Telling it Again and Again: Repetition in Literature and Film* (Ithaca, N.Y.: Cornell University Press, 1972) p. 4.
10. F. R. and Q. D. Leavis, *Dickens the Novelist* (New York: Random House, 1970) p. 311.
11. Henri Bergson, 'Laughter', p. 71.
12. See Dickens's speech to the Birmingham Polytechnic Institute, 28 February 1844, p. 61 in K. J. Fielding's edition of the *Speeches*, in which Dickens expresses the fear that 'those who labour day by day, surrounded by machinery, might be permitted to degenerate into machines themselves'. See also Herbert Sussman, *Victorians and the Machine* (Cambridge, Mass.: Harvard University Press, 1968), and Leo Marx, *The Machine in the Garden* (New York and London: Oxford University Press, 1964).
13. This is Steven Marcus's phrase, although he uses it to describe tableaux such as that of Fagin in the courtroom, surrounded by eyes.
14. Like Freud, Dickens recognised that only change or contrasts could cause sensation. Or as D. G. Garan says in *The Paradox of Pleasure and Relativity: The Psychological Causal Law* (New York: Philosophical Library, 1963) p. 55: 'Everybody has noticed that a green insect is not seen in the grass, that a noise is not heard amidst similar noises, that an odour in the air is not noticed if it persists for long, and so on. . . . As has finally been recognised by psychology, only change can give sensation.'
15. See Mary McCarthy, 'Recalled to Life, or Charles Dickens at the Bar', in *On the Contrary* (New York: Farrar, Straus & Cudahy, 1946) for a discussion of the Victorian love of extremes, the 'passion for mountain-climbing, for gorges and precipices, for the abysmal vertigo of crime and innocence, horror and bathos'.
16. See John Crowe Ransom, *The World's Body* (Baton Rouge: Louisiana State

University Press, 1968) p. 290. 'We find ourselves sometimes possessed of powerful feeling and yet cannot quite tell what actions they want of us; or find ourselves even learning to enjoy the pangs of feeling, in the conceited consciousness that they are our very own, and therefore reluctant to resolve them in action, and taking a perverse pleasure in stirring them up, like a harrowing of hell.'

17. Alexander Welsh, *The City of Dickens* (Oxford: Clarendon Press, 1971) p. 28.
18. Steven Marcus, 'Human Nature, Social Orders, and 19th Century Systems of Explanation: Starting in with George Eliot', in *Salmagundi*, No. 28 (Winter 1975) p. 22.
19. Pearl Chester Solomon, *Dickens and Melville in their Time* (New York and London: Columbia University Press, 1975) p. 3.

7 ONE READER READING

1. James Kincaid, *Dickens and the Rhetoric of Laughter* (Oxford: Clarendon Press, 1971) p. 77.
2. J. Hillis Miller, *Charles Dickens: The World of His Novels* (Bloomington, Ind.: Indiana University Press, 1969) pp. 95–6.
3. James Kincaid, p. 76.
4. Steven Marcus, *Dickens: From Pickwick to Dombey* (London: Chatto & Windus, 1965) p. 147.
5. Geoffrey Tillotson, *A View of Victorian Literature* (Oxford: Clarendon Press, 1978) p. 138.
6. Steven Marcus, p. 163.
7. Ibid., p. 159.
8. James Kincaid, p. 95.
9. Steven Marcus, p. 139.
10. Roland Barthes, 'To Write: An Intransitive Verb?', in Richard and Fernande DeGeorge (eds) *The Structuralists From Marx to Lévi-Strauss* (New York: Doubleday Anchor, 1972) p.157.
11. Stanley E. Fish, 'Literature in the Reader', in *Self-Consuming Artifacts* (Berkeley: University of California Press, 1972) p. 404.
12. Edward Said, *Beginnings: Intention and Method* (New York: Basic Books, 1975).
13. James Kincaid, *Dickens and the Rhetoric of Laughter* (Oxford: Clarendon Press, 1971) p. 78.
14. Stanley E. Fish, p. 384.
15. Steven Marcus, 'Human Nature, Social Orders, and 19th Century Systems of Explanation: Starting in with George Eliot', in *Salmagundi*, No. 28 (Winter 1975), pp. 38–41.
16. James Kincaid, p. 77.

Index

Characters are indexed under the names by which they are most commonly referred.

Affery (in *Little Dorrit*), 11, 101, 104, 107

Arnheim, Rudolf, 93

Auden, W. H., 55

Bagehot, Walter, 5, 36

Bagnets, the (in *Bleak House*), 83

Bagstock, Major (in *Dombey and Son*), 22

Barkis (in *David Copperfield*), 100

Barnaby Rudge, 23, 45, 47, 65, 70–1, 73, 87, 106

Barthes, Roland, 113

Bates, Charley (in *Oliver Twist*), 75

Beadnell, Maria, 6

Bergson, Henri, 8, 99–100, 102–3

Blackmur, R. P., 19

Blackpool, Stephen (in *Hard Times*), 75, 86

Bleak House, 33–4, 40, 45, 47, 48–9, 50, 65, 82, 88–9, 93–5, 100, 117

Boffins, the (in *Our Mutual Friend*), 32–3, 50, 69, 83

Booth, Wayne, 28, 51–2, 71

Bounderby (in *Hard Times*), 11, 75, 79, 83, 102

Brass, Foxey (in *The Old Curiosity Shop*), 115

Brown, Mrs (in *Dombey and Son*), 59, 72

Brownlow, Mr (in *Oliver Twist*), 69, 74, 75, 86

Bumble (in *Oliver Twist*), 44, 60, 81

Burdett-Coutts, Baroness Angela, 6, 64

Burke, Kenneth, 25, 59–60, 77–8

Butt, John, 4, 32, 73

Carker, Harriet (in *Dombey and Son*), 66, 80, 84

Carlyle, Thomas, 5, 12, 40, 72, 80–1

Cavalletto, John (in *Little Dorrit*), 26–7, 72, 90

Chambers, Ross, x–xi, 25, 28, 41, 43, 53

Chatman, Seymour, xi, 14, 35

Cheerbyles, the (in *Nicholas Nickelby*), 8

Chesterton, G. K., xii, 1, 39

Chick, Mrs (in *Dombey and Son*), 17–18, 68

Chicken, the (in *Dombey and Son*), 23

Chiverys, the (in *Little Dorrit*), 83

A Christmas Carol, 8

Chuffey, Mr (in *Martin Chuzzlewit*), 105–6

Chuzzlewit, Jonas (in *Martin Chuzzlewit*), 66, 113

Chuzzlewit, Martin Jr (in *Martin Chuzzlewit*), 34–5

Clennam, Arthur (in *Little Dorrit*), 37–9, 50, 63, 70, 82, 84, 85, 86

Clennam, Mrs (in *Little Dorrit*), 48, 106

Commentary, xi, 25, 28, 31, 41–3, 45, 53–4, 110

Copperfield, David (in *David Copperfield*), 51, 55–6, 60, 62, 72, 84, 86, 91, 97, 99, 100, 102, 116

Crisparkle, Septimus (in *The Mystery of Edwin Drood*), 61

Culler, Jonathan, ix, 99–100

Cuttle, Captain (in *Dombey and Son*), 23, 70, 101

Daleski, H. M., 72

Dartle, Rosa (in *David Copperfield*), 51-2, 74

David Copperfield, 42, 55-6, 59, 65-6, 68, 72, 84, 92, 97, 100, 102-3, 106

Dedlock, Lady (in *Bleak House*), 48, 50, 72, 94

Dedlock, Sir Leicester (in *Bleak House*), 102, 106

Description, nature and function of, xi, 8-11, 13, 19-22, 24, 26-30, 35-6, 38-9, 49-53, 79-80, 88-99

Dick, Mr (in *David Copperfield*), 68

Dickens, Catherine, 18, 68

Dickens, Charles
  ambivalences in, 6-9, 68-72, 110-11, 123-4
  and serial publication, 4
  as a child, 39
  as a reporter in court, 25
  escapes from personal problems, 18-19, 64-5, 107
  literary intentions and their execution, 2-8, 12, 18-19, 22, 27-9, 32-4, 36-44, 49, 52-3, 62-5, 67-8, 73, 76-9, 81, 85-7, 90-3, 95-7, 100-102, 104-9, 113-14, 119-21

Dickens, Frederick, 22

Dickens, Henry Fielding, 6

Disharmonies
  between description and repetition, 8-9, 99-109
  between images and rhetorical commentary, xi-xii, 8-11, 25-33, 35-41, 81-99
  between rhetoric and plot, 8-11, 33-5, 37, 40-9, 69, 71, 116-19
  between seems and if, and rhetoric, 9, 12-13, 49-54, 87

Dolls, Mr (in *Our Mutual Friend*), 72, 98

Dombey, Edith (Granger) (in *Dombey and Son*), 4, 19-20, 22, 59, 72, 75, 80, 118

Dombey, Florence (in *Dombey and Son*), 17, 60, 74, 80, 101

Dombey, Paul Sr (in *Dombey and Son*), 16-17, 70, 74-5, 80, 102, 118

Dombey, Paul Jr (in *Dombey and Son*), 16

Dombey and Son, 16-23, 39, 46, 59, 66-7, 69, 80, 84, 100, 101

Dorrit, Mr (in *Little Dorrit*), 82

Doyce, Daniel (in *Little Dorrit*), 85

Dreiser, Theodore, 40-1, 124n

Endell, Martha (in *David Copperfield*), 91-2

Estella (in *Great Expectations*), 4, 68

Fagin (in *Oliver Twist*), 51, 75, 97, 98-9

Fanger, Donald, 91

Faulkner, William, 2, 51-2, 92-3

Fenichel, Otto, 101

Fezziwig (in *A Christmas Carol*), 8

Fibbotson, Mrs (in *David Copperfield*), 58

Finching, Flora (in *Little Dorrit*), 68

Fish, Stanley E., xiii, 114, 119

Flintwinch (in *Little Dorrit*), 60-1, 79, 104

Flite, Miss (in *Bleak House*), 47, 101, 105

Ford, George, 5

Forster, E. M., 1, 74, 77

Forster, John, 4, 6, 17, 18, 39, 64-5, 72

Frye, Northrop, 124n

Gamfield (in *Oliver Twist*), 44, 61, 75, 86

Gamp, Sairey (in *Martin Chuzzlewit*), 57-8, 61, 74

Garan, D. G., 130n

Gargery, Joe (in *Great Expectations*), 82, 101, 105

Gargery, Mrs Joe (in *Great Expectations*), 30, 105

Garis, Robert, 41-2, 88

Garland, Mr (in *The Old Curiosity Shop*), 119

Gashford, Mr (in *Barnaby Rudge*), 23

Gay, Walter (in *Dombey and Son*), 4, 101

General, Mrs (in *Little Dorrit*), 104

Genette, Gérard, 42

Gills, Sol (in *Dombey and Son*), 70

Girard, René, xiii

Gogol, Nicolai, 57-8

Goodman, Paul, 47-9

Gradgrind, Thomas (in *Hard Times*), 83

Great Expectations, 59, 67, 82, 106

Guerard, Albert, xii–xiii

Gummidge, Mrs (in *David Copperfield*), 68, 101–102

Halliday, M. A. K., ix

Ham (in *David Copperfield*), 84

Hard Times, 53, 79, 80, 83, 102, 107

Hardy, Barbara, xii, 33, 71

Haredale, Geoffrey (in *Barnaby Rudge*), 23

Harmon (Rokesmith), John (in *Our Mutual Friend*), 74, 76, 83–4

Harris, Mrs (in *Martin Chuzzlewit*), 57

Harthhouse, James (in *Hard Times*), 83

Hartman, Geoffrey, 77

Harvey, William, 78, 91

Havisham, Miss (in *Great Expectations*), 30, 68, 105–6

Headstone, Bradley (in *Our Mutual Friend*), 98, 104

Heep, Uriah (in *David Copperfield*), 11, 103–4

Hexam, Gaffer (in *Our Mutual Friend*), 33, 61, 127n

Hexam, Lizzie (in *Our Mutual Friend*), 74, 98

Higden, Betty (in *Our Mutual Friend*), 32–3, 69, 75, 83, 86, 104

Hirn, Hrjo, 76

Holland, Norman N., 32, 77, 99

Horton, Susan R., xiii

House, Humphry, 30

Hugh of Maypole (in *Barnaby Rudge*), 70

Humphrey, Master (in *The Old Curiosity Shop*), 112, 114

Iser, Wolfgang, xiii, 4, 37

Jaggers, Mr (in *Great Expectations*), 12, 103

Jakobson, Roman, ix–x

Jarley, Mrs (in *The Old Curiosity Shop*), 116

Jellyby, Mr (in *Bleak House*), 12, 83, 103

Jingle, Alfred (in *Pickwick Papers*), 128n

Jo (in *Bleak House*), 40

Johnson, Edgar, 6, 18

Johnson, Samuel, 27

Joram (in *David Copperfield*), 62

Kawin, Bruce, 103

Kermode, Frank, xiii

Kincaid, James, 45, 61, 110–11, 119, 121, 127n

Krook (in *Bleak House*), 52, 79, 97

Krutch, Joseph Wood, 83

Kuhn, Thomas, xi–xii

Lang, Berel, x

Leavis, F. R. and Q. D., 33, 34–5, 39, 41–2, 62–3, 103

Lesser, Simon, 29, 31, 75, 100

Lewes, George Henry, 48

Lightwood, Mortimer (in *Our Mutual Friend*), 51, 127n

Lister, T. H., 36

Little Dorrit (Amy) (in *Little Dorrit*), 35, 48, 50, 56, 59, 68, 75, 82–3, 86, 104

Little Dorrit, 26–8, 35–7, 39, 41–2, 43, 48, 49, 52, 59, 60, 62–3, 65, 78–9, 82, 84–5, 90, 100, 104, 106–7, 114–17

Little Em'ly (in *David Copperfield*), 68, 84, 97, 102

Little Nell (in *The Old Curiosity Shop*), 56, 66, 69, 83, 112, 120–1

Lorry, Jarvis (in *A Tale of Two Cities*), 95

Mack, Maynard, 127n

Maggy (in *Little Dorrit*), 59

Magwitch (in *Great Expectations*), 11, 30, 86, 103

Manette, Lucie (in *A Tale of Two Cities*), 95

Manette, Mr (in *A Tale of Two Cities*), 49

Manning, Sylvia Bank, 62–3

Marcus, Steven, 14, 15, 29, 64, 88, 109, 110–11, 120

Martin Chuzzlewit, 34, 55, 61, 66, 73, 105

Marwood, Alice (in *Dombey and Son*), 59, 75, 80
Marx, Leo, 67, 81
Maylie, Harry (in *Oliver Twist*), 87
Maylie, Rose (in *Oliver Twist*), 60, 75, 80, 87
M'Choakumchild (in *Hard Times*), 80
Meagles, Mr (in *Little Dorrit*), 27–8, 41–2, 85
Meagles, Pet (in *Little Dorrit*), 27, 41–2, 82
Mell, Mr (in *David Copperfield*), 56
Melville, Herman, 13, 19, 116, 124n
Merdle, Mr (in *Bleak House*), 103
Merdle, Mrs (in *Bleak House*), 79
Micawbers, the (in *David Copperfield*), 68, 100–1
Miller, J. Hillis, 14, 110
Milvey, Rev (in *Our Mutual Friend*), 56–7
Monks (in *Oliver Twist*), 72, 75, 82, 113
Murdstones, the (in *David Copperfield*), 68, 75, 97
The Mystery of Edwin Drood, 13, 49, 61, 66

Nancy (in *Oliver Twist*), 60, 69, 75, 80, 98
narration, xi, 20, 29, 41, 43–51, 117–19
Nicholas Nickleby, xii, 8, 22, 42, 44, 61, 73, 110
Nickleby, Ralph (in *Nicholas Nickleby*), 8
Nubbles, Kit (in *The Old Curiosity Shop*), 112, 115

The Old Curiosity Shop, 73, 83, 97–8, 110–21
Oliver Twist, 11, 42, 44, 46, 48, 51, 59, 60, 63–4, 65, 73, 75, 80, 81, 82, 86, 90–1, 97, 106, 107–8, 110
Omer (in *David Copperfield*), 62
Orwell, George, 74, 95–6
Our Mutual Friend, xii, 32–3, 50–1, 56–7, 69, 70, 79, 82, 85, 98, 100, 104, 106

Pancks (in *Little Dorrit*), 82, 84, 104

Pardiggle, Mrs (in *Bleak House*), 82
Pecksniff, Mr (in *Martin Chuzzlewit*), 11, 50, 103–4
Peggottys, the (in *David Copperfield*), 55, 83, 91–2, 101, 102, 106
Pickwick, Mr (in *Pickwick Papers*), 70
Pickwick Papers, 57–8, 70, 73
Pinch, Tom (in *Martin Chuzzlewit*), 66
Pip (in *Great Expectations*), 4, 30, 82, 101, 105
Plornishes, the (in *Little Dorrit*), 83–4
Pocket, Herbert (in *Great Expectations*), 59
Podsnaps, the (in *Our Mutual Friend*), 75, 95, 104
Praz, Mario, 1
Pross, Miss (in *A Tale of Two Cities*), 59
Pumblechook, Mr (in *Great Expectations*), 30

Quilp, Daniel (in *The Old Curiosity Shop*), 111, 114, 120

Ransom, John Crowe, 28–9, 108
Readers
  ambivalent responses to Dickens's novels, 71, 84–5, 103–6
  demands as audience, 8
  formal expectations of Dickens's novels, 9–11, 13, 15, 45, 58
  making meaning from Dickens's novels, xiii, 8–9, 14–16, 18–20
  response decisions, 23–4, 25, 32–3, 36–7, 43, 47, 50–7, 59, 81, 92–9, 103–4, 107–9
  source of readers' responses, 2, 9, 11, 14, 20, 52–4, 58–9, 61–3, 76–8, 87, 97–8, 111–12, 114–15, 119–20
  repetition, 8, 11, 12, 99–109
Richards, I. A., 1, 90
Riderhood, Rogue (in *Our Mutual Friend*), 51–2, 85, 98
Rigaud (in *Little Dorrit*), 26–7, 43, 70, 72, 90
Ruskin, John, 24

Said, Edward, 115
Sapsea, Mrs (in *The Mystery of Edwin Drood*), 61

Scott, Sir Walter, 5
Scrooge (in *A Christmas Carol*), 8
Shaw, George Bernard, 7, 40, 96
Sikes, Bill (in *Oliver Twist*), 75, 98
Sketches by Boz, 49, 52
Slackbridge (in *Hard Times*), 53, 87
Sloppy (in *Our Mutual Friend*), 104
Snagsby, Mr (in *Bleak House*), 93–5
Solomon, Pearl Chester, 8, 109
Sowerberry, Mr (in *Oliver Twist*), 86
Spenlow, Dora (in *David Copperfield*), 82
Spitzer, Leo, ix
Sprodgkin, Mrs (in *Our Mutual Friend*), 56–7
Squod, Phil (in *Bleak House*), 45
Steerforth, James (in *David Copperfield*), 84, 102, 127n
Stoehr, Taylor, 87
Sucksmith, Harvey P., 26–7, 45, 52
Summerson, Esther (in *Bleak House*), 33, 40, 50–1, 65, 70, 72, 82–3, 86
Sussman, Herbert, 130n
Swiveller, Dick (in *The Old Curiosity Shop*), 118

Taine, H. A., 78
A Tale of Two Cities, 44, 49, 50, 52, 59, 98
Tapley, Mark (in *Martin Chuzzlewit*), 44
Tappertit, Simon (in *Barnaby Rudge*), 23, 87, 104
Tattycoram (in *Little Dorrit*), 27, 41–2, 52
Tillotson, Geoffrey, 30, 110
Tillotson, Kathleen, 4, 32, 73
Tippins, Lady (in *Our Mutual Friend*), 79

Toots, Mr (in *Dombey and Son*), 23, 101
Towlinson (in *Dombey and Son*), 21
Tox, Miss (in *Dombey and Son*), 17, 23, 67, 74
Trotwood, Betsey (in *David Copperfield*), 55, 68
Tulkinghorn, Mr (in *Bleak House*), 46, 48, 94–5
The Uncommercial Traveller, 22

Varden, Gabriel (in *Barnaby Rudge*), 70, 74
Veneerings, the (in *Our Mutual Friend*), 95

Wade, Miss (in *Little Dorrit*), 41, 52–3, 82
Watson, Hon. Mrs R., 6
Wegg, Silas (in *Our Mutual Friend*), 69, 79, 82
Weller, Sam (in *Pickwick Papers*), 57–8
Welsh, Alexander, xii, 7, 67, 107
Wemmick, Mr (in *Great Expectations*), 67, 82–3
Wickfields, the (in *David Copperfield*), 55, 68
Wilfer, Bella (in *Our Mutual Friend*), 50, 74, 83–4
Wilfer, Mrs (in *Our Mutual Friend*), 12, 82, 106
Wilfer, Pa (in *Our Mutual Friend*), 83
Willett, John (in *Barnaby Rudge*), 106
Wrayburn, Eugene (in *Our Mutual Friend*), 51, 74, 98, 127n
Wren, Jenny (in *Our Mutual Friend*), 68, 72, 74, 83